gardening
& planting
by the
mo●n
2014

gardening
& planting
by the
mo●n
2014

nick kollerstrom

quantum
LONDON • NEW YORK • TORONTO • SYDNEY

quantum

An imprint of W. Foulsham & Co. Ltd
Capital Point, 33 Bath Road, Slough, Berkshire SL1 3UF, England

Foulsham books can be found in all good bookshops and direct from
www.foulsham.com

Dedicated to the memory of Frau Maria Thun, pioneer of lunar gardening

ISBN: 978-0-572-04416-9

A CIP record for this book is available from the British Library

Printed and bound by CPI Group (UK) Ltd, Croydon, CR0 4YY

Contents

The pull of the Moon is considerable. Not only does it move tides twice a day, it pulls on the Earth. Many gardeners and farmers are rediscovering the benefit of planting according to its phases, part of a profound knowledge neglected by modern techniques.

Harmony, A New Way of Looking at our World, by HRH The Prince of Wales, with Tony Juniper and Ian Skelly, 2010, p.137.

Introduction

To everything there is a season and a time to every purpose under heaven: a time to be born and a time to die: a time to plant, and a time to pluck up what is planted ...

Ecclesiastes 3:1–2

very gardener and farmer wants the best possible crops, and we all try out various ways of achieving that end. Since you are reading this, you must have wondered whether you could get better results if you planted in harmony with the cycles of the Moon – I believe you can.

For as long as anyone can remember, people have held a belief in the efficacy of such a practice, and various different traditions have developed. In many countries today, lunar calendars are available for farmers and gardeners, and there is considerable evidence to show that crops can benefit from the correct use of a lunar gardening guide. It is our hope that this manual will come to be used not only for its practical advantages, but also as an inspiration to gardeners to become more aware of the life-rhythms in nature, which mysteriously connect the growth of plants with cosmic time-cycles.

The aim of the book is not only to provide detailed planting and gardening advice, but also to stimulate interest in, and research into, the question of lunar influence, within the context of the burgeoning organic movement. Those who simply wish to apply the recommended gardening advice for 2014 can turn straight to the calendar pages.

Current lunar gardening guides often disagree on many of their recommendations. Old traditions have grown confused with the passage of time, and a new attitude has appeared, within the twentieth-century organic movement, known as bio-dynamics. The bio-dynamic movement was founded in 1924 by the Austrian teacher and philosopher Rudolf Steiner (1861–1925), the founder of the anthroposophical movement. It attempts to use holistic principles, viewing the farm as an integral whole and taking account of the condition of the cosmos. The recommendations here may not be the same as those in other lunar gardening guides, but they may have a better chance of producing dependable crop improvements.

Gardeners work with time. They continually make judgements on how the seasons are progressing, what the weather may do, and so on, always in the context of having limited time available. Gardening and farming, however, can take on an extra dimension if one is aware that, besides these practical considerations, there are also basic cycles of the heavens to which animals and the plant world are attuned. Plants receive their energy for growth from the Sun but, in other more subtle ways, they are continually affected by the Moon's ever-changing rhythms. A decision as to when to plant a tree should take such lunar cycles into account, just as a sailor puts to sea only when the tides are right.

During the twentieth century, systematic experiments began to determine how the various lunar cycles played a part in plant metabolism, growth and development. Certain keys to understanding the relationship of plant responses to lunar influence have now emerged and can be incorporated into a gardener's or farmer's plans as to when best to carry out various tasks, in particular sowing, planting and harvesting. I wish to express deep gratitude towards Simon Best: he and I composed *Planting by the Moon* in 1980, and worked with it through the 1980s, as a synthesis of time-honoured traditions and twentieth-century research. Its basic ideas are here slightly developed.

There is also mounting evidence that the lunar cycle, particularly the Full Moon and the lunar nodes, has a considerable effect on horse breeding. This is explained in more detail on pages 37–38 and I hope in further years to integrate this information into the calendar.

Various astrological and related concepts are used in the calendar, but readers unfamiliar with such things need not worry: this book provides clear, step-by-step explanations, highlighting both the continuous rhythms of energy that ebb and flow and should resonate with the sympathetic worker, and also the specific moments, or celestial events, which the gardener should endeavour to catch.

Those who use ephemerides or astrology programs may notice that the Moon sign entries in our diary differ from those they will find there. This is because astrological programs use the tropical zodiac, whereas ours use the sidereal calendar, indicating where the star constellations are, and the systems differ by two days of the Moon's motions. This is explained on page 15.

This calendar also gives dates for the 'Moons of celebration', the sacred Moons of the Muslim, Jewish, Hindu and Chinese New Years, and the Full Moon of May, which the Buddhists celebrate a month after the Full Moon that fixes Easter. It also includes the 12 lunar months of the Muslim year.

To extend the usefulness of the calendar to new buyers, it also includes a full 15 months of diary pages.

If you want to look at some of the evidence in support of the recommendations given here, there is a website collecting experimental results: www.considera.org. It is encouraging that someone is collecting the raw data of these experiments and let's hope that continues. Plants are so sensitive to these subtle influences, as science is just beginning to discover. Also, a couple of my published articles on the subject are on the UK Biodynamic website at: www.biodynamic.org.uk/Research.htm#Mares%20fertility. One of these shows how very much horses respond to the lunar month – as, one assumes, do all living creatures. You will find an index of all Nick Kollerstrom's research, including planting by the moon, at www.astrozero.co.uk/astroscience/koll2indx.htm

Perspectives

Pleiades rising in the dawning sky,
   Harvest is nigh.
Pleiades setting in the waning night,
   Ploughing is right.
Forty days and nights in the turning year
   They disappear.
When they shine again in the morning shade,
   Sharpen your blade.

Hesiod, *Works and Days*, eighth century BC

lants are adapted to the primary cycles of time – the day, month and year. This book focuses on the second of these, the monthly rhythms that are so important for the plant world. These monthly cycles are lunar, in contrast with the day and year, which are solar. It may be a mystery as to how plants respond to these monthly cycles, but that doesn't stop them from being of practical value in the garden and on the farm.

The sensitivity of plants to minute levels of energy was first systematically studied by the Indian scientist Sir Jagadis Chandra Bose (1858–1937) in the early years of the twentieth century. Using carefully designed apparatus, he produced a mass of evidence showing that plants have a far greater capacity to respond to subtle environmental stimuli than had previously been believed.

Plants, small animals and birds are attuned to the natural electric and magnetic fields of the Earth. By altering such fields in the laboratory, scientists have been able to alter the rate and other characteristics of a plant's growth as well as the direction in which a bird will fly. The Earth's geomagnetic field has been shown to vary with the lunar month and to bring about some large-scale effects.

The Biosphere

One of the first lunar-cycle effects to be clearly demonstrated was in rainfall. This was reported in 1962 by two independent groups of researchers, one in the northern and one in the southern hemisphere. Their results appeared in *Science* magazine – in the same issue, for mutual support! The rhythm of the Moon's pull on the sea causes tides to reach their highest twice a month, on average a day after the Full and New Moons. Average rainfall also follows this twice-monthly rhythm, peaking three or four days after the Full and New Moons. The two groups of researchers examined 50 years of data and found that the magnitude of the lunar effect they had discovered varied with the level of solar activity.

The Earth's magnetic field is a membrane that shields us from solar radiation. We know that it pulsates to a monthly rhythm, strengthening following the Full Moon. The geomagnetic field stays low for the week before the Full Moon, then it increases sharply, remaining high for some days.

Thunderstorms recorded by Eastern US weather stations over the years 1942–65 followed a pattern similar to that seen in the geomagnetism data. They decreased for a few days before the Full Moon, and then increased sharply, peaking two days after the Full Moon. Conversely, there was a definite decrease on days following the New Moon. In contrast, a survey of hurricanes and typhoons in the North Atlantic, from 80 years of data, found they tended to occur 20 per cent more frequently on days following both the Full and New Moons.

So, the biosphere as a whole responds to this fundamental cycle. The effect of this pulsation upon climate is slowly becoming recognised as science, not just folklore. The changing Sun–Moon angle causes huge electric and magnetic changes in the upper atmosphere. It is therefore little more than common sense to affirm that both gardeners and farmers should take notice of it.

Traditional Lore

There is a wide but fragmentary body of folk-knowledge, gleaned from many cultures and various ages, that reflects the age-old belief of farmers and gardeners that the Moon somehow influences the growth of their crops.

Hesiod, the Greek astronomer and contemporary of Homer, is considered to have written the first lunar agricultural manual, in the eighth century. His poem *Works and Days* advised farmers on how to regulate many activities by the phases of the Moon. Later, this emphasis on the lunar phases became particularly important to Roman farmers. Lunar-planting rules were recorded by Cato and Pliny. The primary rules, many of which have persisted in folklore to this day, focus on the differences between the effects of the waxing and waning Moon.

This same view was current in seventeenth-century England: *'he* [the farmer] *shall gather and carry into his house whatsoever he would have to endure and last long, at such times as the Moone shall decrease'* (La Maison Rustique, 1616).

Basically, whatever required growth was started during the waxing phase, and whatever needed to dry, cure or decrease without decay was dealt with in the waning phase. The dark time just before the New Moon was said to be especially favourable for the latter activities. Thus, planting crops, picking grapes for wine and shearing sheep were carried out during the waxing Moon, and general harvesting of crops, felling timber and castration of animals during the waning phase.

Pliny was a keen observer of nature, shown by his multi-volume *History of Nature*. He believed he could discern how, *'that tiny creature the ant, at the Moon's conjunction keeps quite quiet, but at full Moon works busily even in the nights'.* If there was a problem with the ground being damp, then Pliny's advice was to sow seeds in the waning half of the lunar cycle so that the land could dry out. Seventeenth-century British gardening guides quoted Pliny on this subject.

The various facets of lunar lore were transmitted, both verbally and in scattered writings, down through the ages and across cultures to the present day, although modern collections of these adages markedly illustrate the confusion of ideas in this area. Grafting and planting-out operations should be performed during the waxing Moon because rising sap is said to help the formation of new shoots or the establishment of a new graft. Lawns are said to benefit from being sown during the waxing phase, a time also propitious for transplanting trees and flowers. One of the oldest maxims that recommended using the waxing/waning division with respect to planting is as follows: crops which produce their yield above ground should be planted during the waxing Moon, whereas those that produce below ground should be sown during the waning Moon. This idea can be found in many parts of the world, but so can similar ideas which modify or contradict it.

In particular, it is claimed that sowing around the Full or New Moon will improve crop growth. Here again opinions vary; for example, some advocate planting in the days immediately preceding the New Moon so that seeds will have germinated and be ready to grow as the Moon begins to increase. More widespread is the opposite opinion, that crops should be sown just before the Full Moon. This is the view particularly associated with the work of Lili Kolisko, who came to Britain from Germany in 1936. The results of her years of study were published in 1938-9, and claimed that seed germination, and especially the unfolding of the first leaves of young shoots, pointed to the days prior to Full Moon as an optimal sowing time, and those prior to New Moon as the worst, in terms of speed of growth.

However, although Moon phase does affect plant metabolism, there is little reliable evidence that sowing at any particular point in the lunar-phase cycle will influence the final yield. Seedling germination and growth may increase around and especially just before the Full Moon, but such effects may not show up in the final crop yield. Much of the confusion of traditional belief may have arisen from such a confounding of different aspects of plant growth.

More recently, it used to be a common custom in the west of England to gather in the 'hoard fruit' in the 'shrinking of the Moon'. Apples bruised in the harvesting would then tend to preserve better over the winter. This accords with modern studies showing varying plant water-absorption at the different phases, suggesting that some facets of lunar lore may be vindicated by modern research.

The Four Elements

Although modern lunar gardening guides tend to disagree on many issues, they do concur on one point: they all use a notion of dividing the zodiac into four periods, each connected with a particular element – Earth, Air, Fire and Water.

At the core of this calendar is a four-element pattern, generated by the motion of the Moon against the stars, a modern system, based on an ancient idea, that has been in use for several decades and is now proving its usefulness and accuracy.

Each month, the Moon moves around the sky against the 12 constellations of the zodiac, each of which has its particular affinity with one of the four elements.

Each of the elements has three constellations linked to it, and these are spaced equally around the circle of the zodiac. The diagram below shows the sky-triangles, or trigons, that map the three related signs. The 27-day orbit of the Moon against the stars means that each element lasts for two or three days and is repeated every nine days. The elements of Earth, Water, Air and Fire are said to influence the growth and performance of a particular sort of plant, respectively Root, Leaf, Flower and Fruit-seed. Further division into the well-known 12 signs of the zodiac is secondary in this scheme.

The four-element theory was first expressed by Empedocles in the fifth century BC in Sicily. He believed that nature used the four elements – fire, wind, sea and stone – to paint with, just as an artist uses four colours. The ancient Greeks also applied the four-element theory in their four temperaments, much used in their medical practice, defining people's characters by their related element.

There are further parallels in other areas of knowledge. Physicists work with 12 types of 'fundamental' particles and four states of matter – solid, liquid, gas and plasma (hot, and above the atmosphere). Biochemists describe four types of code in the DNA strand, while Jungian psychology talks of four temperaments.

The four-element cycle underlying the zodiac

The theory is that in nature there are four kinds of subtle energy, 'formative forces', which work to influence the way a plant will develop, linking the time of sowing to the final condition of the crop when harvested. These forces are activated by the Moon's passage through the zodiac-elements, as the seed is sown. This pattern of influence is to do with the pattern of the stars rather than the zodiac used in modern astrology.

The Star Rhythm

The sequence of element days, the star rhythm, runs: Root days, Flower days, Leaf days and then Fruit-seed days.

Root days are the times to sow carrots, potatoes, radishes and other root crops. These days occur when the Moon passes in front of the stars of one of three planets linked to the Earth element: Taurus, Virgo and Capricorn. When this happens, the

Moon is said to have an Earth-type energy. If the weather is unsuitable for sowing those particular crops, simply wait for the next set of Root days nine days later.

Root days relate to the Earth signs   *Taurus*   *Virgo*   *Capricorn*

Leaf days are times when the Moon is in front of the constellations related to Water – Cancer, Scorpio and Pisces – and is the time to sow lettuce, cabbage and other leafy crops.

Leaf days relate to the Water signs   *Cancer*   *Scorpio*   *Pisces*

Flower days relate to the Air signs – Gemini, Libra and Aquarius – and are the best times to sow broccoli, globe artichoke, cauliflowers and similar plants.

Flower days relate to the Air signs   *Gemini*   *Libra*   *Aquarius*

Fruit-seed days relate to the Fire signs – Aries, Leo and Sagittarius – and are ideal for sowing tomatoes, beans and peas.

Fruit-seed days relate to the Fire signs   *Aries*   *Leo*   *Sagittarius*

One can visualise this as a sequence of plant development. First the root descends into the soil (Earth), then the leaves unfold, with water flowing up the stem and transpiring out through the leaves (Water). Then come the flowers, emitting their fragrance to attract bees and butterflies to fertilise them (Air). Lastly, the flowers fall away as the heat of the summer shrivels up the plant, drying it into the final stage of the seed (Fire). The tiny seeds contain the essence of the flower, just as fire is the least material or least dense of the four elements. Biologically, one may prefer to view the last stage as Warmth rather than Fire, emphasising its constructive role in a process of maturation.

This element cycle, linked to the stars and therefore known as a sidereal rhythm (from the Latin word for star, *sidera*), is one of the two fundamental lunar cycles relevant for a lunar-gardening calendar. The other is the better-known waxing-waning lunar month of 29.5 days, which influences fertility, germination, water absorption and metabolism. The chapter covering the Moon and crop yield (see page 27) looks at the evidence for this element cycle affecting living things, and why a modern grower should take notice of it. It appears especially relevant to organic growers who wish to work in harmony with the living rhythms of the Earth, as it seems to require a 'living' soil for the element rhythm to work; whereas, lunar-phase effects will turn up anywhere!

Belief in the Moon's influence on the fertility of plants was once firmly embedded in the consciousness of ancient people. As science rediscovers these subtle links between earth and sky, farmers are again coming to regard the application of lunar cycles as a sensible and valuable practice.

Frau Maria Thun

This year's book is dedicated to the memory of Maria Thun, 1922–2012, pioneer of the modern lunar gardening calendar. For forty years, she and her family produced a calendar that was translated into over twenty languages every year. It sold over a hundred thousand copies without advertising or promotion, its use spreading by word of mouth. Her various books show her creative investigation of the subject, and how she tested better ways for organic growers. In my opinion her calendar really worked, which is why she will be remembered. Maria discovered the basic four-element rhythm: Empedocles discovered the four elements, Vettius Valens put them into the Zodiac, and Maria Thun discovered plant response to them.

Inevitably the question of why we produce this calendar must arise, if hers was so good? With no disrespect let me itemise five differences. Firstly, this book uses the correct and optimal zodiac for agricultural use, namely the star-zodiac which is called 'sidereal'. Her calendar used the very imbalanced Bio-dynamic zodiac. A herb-grower once told me he preferred my calendar because it gave him more time for herbs: the air element (flower-days) is greatly shortened in the Thun calendar, whereas the Root-days get an undue amount of time. Second, I use the cycle of the Moon, as it waxes and wanes, this being fundamental to the gardener's month. Third, I have never been convinced by the 'ascending' and 'descending' Moon, which is used in the B-D calendar so we don't here use that cycle, which pertains to how long the Moon stays above the horizon each day. Fourth, my calendar recommends using Moon aspects to Venus and Saturn; those are the only two planets we use, for fairly traditional reasons, whereas the Thun calendar used other planets such as Mercury and Pluto, I never knew why. Lastly, my calendar uses the hour of moonrise, coming from a British tradition of lunar-gardening.

One thing this calendar doesn't do, which hers always did, is give monthly weather and climate predictions for the farmer. That is a middle-European tradition, based upon her assessing the balance of planets in the four elements of the Zodiac. Maybe British weather is too variable for such schemes to work here, and I never had confidence in making such predictions.

Both of our calendars are within the European Bio-dynamic tradition and let's hope they can get along together! This calendar was put together by Simon Best and myself in the 1980s, integrating the Bio-dynamic experience with British folk-tradition and scientific investigation. Over the last thirty years it has been encouraging to receive testimonials from calendar-users as to how they have found it works. The Bio-dynamic textbook *Cosmos Earth and Nutrition* (2009) by Richard Thornton-Smith has concluded that farming calendars ought to be using the equal-interval zodiac here advocated, rather than the irregular one used up till now by Bio-Dynamic calendars.

Cycles of the Sky

Time faire, to sowe or to gather be bold,
but set or remove when the weather is cold.
Cut all thing or gather, the Moone in the wane,
but sowe in encreasing, or give it his bane.

Thomas Tusser, *Five Hundred Points of Good Husbandry*, 1573

s we look at the stars scattered across the night sky and the ever-changing face of the Moon, we cannot but be struck by a sense of the primal mystery of the cosmos and wonder if we are linked to it in some fundamental way.

The Moon has four basic monthly cycles, and these describe its motion in relation to the Sun (synodic), to the stars (sidereal), to the Earth (apogee-perigee) and to the ecliptic plane (nodal).

The Synodic or Phase Cycle — Moon and Sun

As the Moon waxes and wanes each month, it mirrors the Sun's light from different angles and appears to increase and decrease in size. It takes 29.5 days to do this. When Full, the Moon is opposite to the Sun in the sky, so that as it rises, the Sun sets. The four positions of the Full, New and quarter Moons each month are shown in the calendar. There are usually 12 Full Moons in a year.

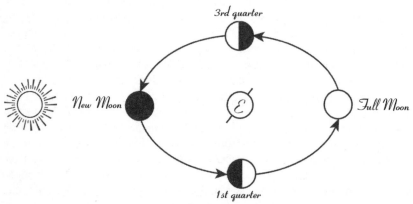

The synodic or phase cycle

The Sun and Moon meet together in the sky at New Moon, when it becomes impossible to see the Moon for several days because it is so close to the Sun. The Greek word *synodos* means 'meeting' and also signified copulation, pointing to the deep connection this cycle has to germination and fertility.

The Sidereal Cycle — Moon and Stars

Once in 27.3 days, the Moon orbits the Earth against the fixed stars. In this time, called a sidereal month, the Moon returns to the same part of the heavens as seen from Earth. It also revolves on its own axis in this same period so that its 'face' is always directed towards the Earth.

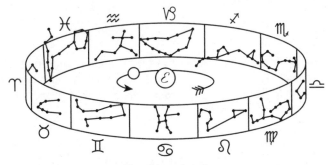

The sidereal cycle

The Moon moves against the same background of constellations as the other planets. It orbits around the Earth in a plane similar to that in which the Earth and planets orbit around the Sun (called the ecliptic). The constellations against which the Moon and planets are seen to move are therefore of special importance. Since ancient times they have been regarded as divided into the 12 constellations of the zodiac. The Moon therefore spends two to three days in each zodiacal constellation. This cycle has a special link with the four elements, as these are related to the signs of the zodiac.

The Apogee–Perigee Cycle — Moon and Earth

The Moon moves around the Earth in an elliptical orbit, so its distance from the Earth varies considerably through the month. Every 27.2 days it reaches its apogee, furthest away from the Earth, then draws closest at its perigee, when it appears larger in the sky, pulls on the tides more strongly, and appears to move faster against the stars. This means that the time that the Moon spends in each of the 12 zodiacal divisions varies by more than 30 per cent in a single rotation. At perigee, the Moon is moving fastest against the stars, and it takes only two days to pass through one zodiacal division, whereas at apogee, when moving slowest, it takes almost three days.

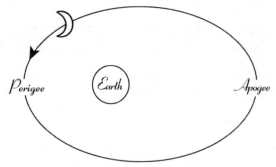

The apogee–perigee cycle

This cycle cannot be seen in the sky, as the apparent change in the size of the Moon is too small to notice. Its effect can be seen in the calendar, however, as the Moon spends the least time moving through a sign at perigee, and the longest at apogee.

The Nodal Cycle – Moon and Ecliptic Plane

The planets revolve around the Sun in approximately the same plane, the ecliptic, and the Moon's orbit is tilted at a slight angle, about 5° to this plane. This means that each month the moon rises above and then sinks below the ecliptic. The two points at which it crosses the ecliptic are called nodes. When moving from south to north of the ecliptic, the Moon reaches its north node, and when moving from north to south, its south node.

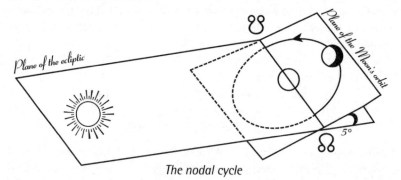

The nodal cycle

The name ecliptic comes from the fact that eclipses happen when Sun, Moon and Earth are in line and on this plane. When the Moon becomes New close to a node, there will be a solar eclipse, and when it becomes Full close to a node, there will be a lunar eclipse. A solar eclipse draws a thin pencil of darkness on the Earth, where its zone of totality is confined. A lunar eclipse, in contrast, is a reddish shadow that passes across the Moon and is visible from half the Earth.

The north and south nodes were called dragon's head and dragon's tail respectively, indicating a belief that they were two special power points in the Moon's orbit – as if a menacing dragon were curled round the zodiac, liable to swallow the Sun at some unpredictable moment. A traditional British gardening guide advised people to avoid sowing seeds over the dragon's tail, the south node. This calendar, in common with bio-dynamic calendars, makes no distinction between these two lunar moments, avoiding both for its sowing times.

The Moon Riding High

How high does the Moon climb in the sky each night? The winter Full Moons are almost overhead, whereas through the summer they hang low above the horizon. On one day each month the Moon arcs highest across the sky, remaining above the horizon for the longest time, then a fortnight later it sinks to its lowest height above the horizon. There is a strong US lunar-gardening tradition that refers to these two halves of the month as 'riding high' and 'riding low'. The effect is very latitude-dependent so that readers in more northern countries will find this cycle more pronounced. For example, in Scotland the Moon hardly sets at one end of the month, then a fortnight later it hardly rises.

This monthly cycle mirrors the Sun's annual journey: in mid-winter the Sun remains low above the horizon, being in front of the stars of Sagittarius, whereas in mid-summer it climbs high in the sky, being in the opposite constellation of Gemini. This cycle fades away near the Equator, then in the southern hemisphere is reversed with both Sun and Moon rising highest against the stars of Sagittarius.

Bio-dynamic calendars also use this cycle, but label it differently. The cycle is split into ascending and descending, according to the height of the Moon above the observer's horizon. The planting out of seedlings is then recommended in the descending half. This cycle is just the 27.3-day star-month, but gets confused with that of the waxing and waning Moon, which may account for similar recommendations being ascribed to the waxing Moon period in British and American folklore.

Harvest Moon

The September Full Moon is called the Harvest Moon. Seen through autumnal mists, it often assumes a yellow hue and, remaining close to the horizon, it appears large in the sky and provides extra hours of illumination – precious to the farmer at this time of year.

At the autumnal equinox, the ecliptic (the path that the planets take round the Sun) is tilted at its least angle to the horizon. So the zodiac belt, containing the orbits of the Moon and planets, runs low above the horizon. This causes the Moon to rise only about 12 minutes later each day – whereas on average throughout the year it rises about 50 minutes later each day. Thus, at this time of harvesting, the Moon continues to rise soon after sunset for a number of successive evenings.

The Harvest Moon was held to be responsible for the ripening of produce and, to the Romans, Diana's day fell at the time of the harvest Full Moon, when offerings were made to her to ensure the ripening of their fruits.

Use of a star-calendar has the advantage that it gives one a motivation for looking at the heavens. Anyone can recognise Orion and the Plough, but what about Taurus and Gemini? In the afterglow of sunset, if the Moon and one or two planets are visible, one can trace the ecliptic as a line through the sky along which the Sun, Moon and planets all travel. Most of what is used in this calendar is visible in the sky above your garden.

Tasting the Wine

Is there a time when wine tastes best? Newspaper headlines affirmed this back in 2009, with the publication of the little book *When Wine Tastes Best* by Maria Thun and her son Matteus. It seems that Fruit days accentuated flavour, while Flower days brought out aromatics. Therefore, half of the zodiac was 'good' for wine tasting. It was recommended that Root days should be avoided for tasting wine – yuk! Traditionally, the vine was ruled by the Sun, and this new finding helps us to appreciate its fiery essence. Headlines claimed, 'Supermarket chains check lunar calendar before inviting critics to drink'. Tesco revealed that it had already been using this method (tasting in the Fire-trigon) for the previous two years. The Wine Society at its annual get-together promoted the idea. One wine-taster said it solved his 'long-standing puzzlement' as to how a wine would taste so much better on certain days.

To test this theory, invest in a 'wine saver' device which is designed to keep a bottle fresh for a few days after it has been opened. There are several such gadgets widely and cheaply available. The Moon moves from Fire (Fruit day) into Earth (Root day) in two or three days, so open the bottle on a Fruit day, then a couple of days later try to remember how it tasted and sample it on a Root day. If you believe it doesn't taste so good, then you have a good reason for planning a party on a Fruit day! It may help to bring out the fiery excitement and sense of fun amongst your guests. While you're at it, why not order some Bio-Dynamic wine to see if it lives up to its reputation? It's said not to give a hangover the next day ...

Using the Star Zodiac

A Doctor too emerged as we proceeded;
No one alive could talk as well as he did
On points of medicine and of surgery,
For, being grounded in astronomy,
He watched his patient's favourable star
And, by his Naturall Magic, knew what are
The lucky hours and planetary degrees
For making charms and magic effigies.

Chaucer, *The Canterbury Tales*

he sidereal zodiac, or zodiac of the stars, is composed of 12 equal 30° divisions – a kind of 'best-fit' of a regular structure upon the irregular constellations of the ecliptic. It is called sidereal to differentiate it from the tropical zodiac that is used by astrologers. It derives from antiquity and, as such, would have been used by the three magi of the New Testament.

In the fifth century BC, the Greek historian Herodotus went to visit the Chaldeans of Mesopotamia, and must have gazed on the fabled hanging gardens of Babylon. These were watered by an extensive, underground irrigation system, where now there is only desert sand. He was mainly impressed by the sheer abundance of their harvests – of grain, figs, olives and vines – and was concerned that the account he gave of them would strain the credulity of his readers.

In that period, 25 centuries ago, the Chaldeans began using the zodiac divisions, dividing the sky into 12 equal sectors to mirror a division of their year into 12 months each containing 30 days. Did the star-wisdom for which the Chaldeans became renowned help them in their harvests? Whereas the modern zodiac is anchored to the seasons of the year, for the Chaldeans it was fixed by various bright stars. They were concerned with what they experienced of the night sky – for example they recorded each time Venus appeared and disappeared from the sky – and perhaps their more experiential attitude could be of value today.

Debates over the star-zodiac's position are only over a degree or so. It is important in some contexts but immaterial for a lunar-gardening calendar. There were certain stars that fixed the zodiac position, in particular Spica, the bright star signifying the sheaf of corn held by the Virgin, around 29° of Virgo. The star-zodiac was used by the astrologers of antiquity in countries around the Mediterranean, until the fifth century AD. A different tradition then developed in the Muslim Arab world using the tropical zodiac, when the two zodiac systems were only a few degrees apart.

The Four Elements – Earth, Air, Fire and Water – had been used in Greek medicine and philosophy for seven centuries until, in the second century AD, after Claudius Ptolemy's time, they were absorbed into the fabric of the zodiac. The sky-triangles (trigons) were thus established, linking the four elements.

Memory of the sidereal zodiac became lost in Europe but continued in India; the zodiac used there is much the same as that understood by the ancient world. Thus the primal star-zodiac, from which the modern tropical zodiac evolved, has been in continuous use for over two millennia. It was rediscovered at the end of the nineteenth century, when clay tablets dug up from the banks of the Tigris were deciphered. A sidereal ephemeris was published in 1981 by Neil Michelson of the US Astro-computing Services. The present calendar uses the same reference as did Michelson, taking the 'Bull's Eye' star Aldebaran as being 15° of Taurus.

In the twentieth century, two incompatible lunar-gardening traditions burgeoned, both ignoring the sidereal zodiac. They offered a choice, of *either* using the tropical zodiac, as favoured nowadays by astrologers, or using 12 unequal constellations, as found in bio-dynamic calendars.

Use of the Tropical Zodiac

The first edition of *Planting by the Moon* explained how the tropical zodiac might be appropriate for human fate, while emphasising that evidence pointed to the sidereal as the right zodiac to use for plant growth:

'Incidentally, we are not implying that astrologers should be using the sidereal zodiac for their work. Rather, it seems that different phenomena may be attuned to different systems. The tropical zodiac is a moving zodiac, moving around 1° every 72 years against the fixed stars, and this evolving system may be valid for man. However, plants are simpler in their organisation than man, and have a far longer history, two factors which seem to have inclined their response to the Moon in terms of the more primal and unchanging sidereal zodiac. The position of the Moon in the tropical zodiac requires calculation, whereas its position in the sidereal zodiac can be observed in the sky. Although plants do not respond to the tropical zodiac divisions, it may well be that man's being is more in tune with the special mathematical treatment of time and space on which the tropical system depends.'

In simple terms: without an ephemeris (a prepared, printed table giving star times and calculations), could one discern when the Moon was entering into a tropical zodiac sign? Certainly not without a most difficult calculation. If we can only do it by calculation, how could one expect the instinctive plant realm to respond to a tropical ingress? In contrast, growers using our calendar have the advantage of being able to see in the sky what is happening in the book.

Agriculturally, the tropical zodiac shows the Sun's journey through the seasons in the northern hemisphere. Thus, the glyph or sign for Aries signifies the young seedling emerging in spring, then the next sign Taurus, the Bull, signifies the vigour of spring. The Sun's entry into Leo at the height of summer indicates its strength there, followed in September by the Virgin as a Ceres figure signifying the harvest. After that comes Libra, as the harvest is measured out; and then the Scorpion signifies the dying and decomposition of nature.

Interpreting the evidence of field experiments in terms of a zodiac framework hinges on the four-element symbolism. Thus, experiments show that root crops such as potato or radish grow better when the Moon is in front of one of the three Earth sectors of the sidereal zodiac. In terms of the tropical zodiac one would have to say that they were growing best when the Moon was in front of one of the three Air signs, because the shift between the two systems is nowadays almost one sign, or about 25°. This would not have the same symbolic significance as associating them with the Earth signs. Likewise it makes more sense to associate leaf crops such as lettuce with Water (sidereal) than with Fire (tropical). The four stages of plant growth – Root, Leaf, Flower and Fruit-seed – are associated with the four elements – Earth, Water, Air and Fire – *only* if a sidereal reference system is used.

The relationship between the sidereal and tropical zodiacs against the constellations

Almanacs based on this 'zodiac of the seasons' – the tropical zodiac – tend to advocate that the three Water signs are fruitful while the three Fire signs are barren, based on straightforward analogy or symbolism. It amounts to viewing only one-quarter of the zodiac as fertile. Sometimes the Earth signs are also admitted to be fertile.

Using the Bio-dynamic Calendar

A major alternative system to the one used here is that used in bio-dynamic calendars. Whereas the sidereal zodiac uses 12 equal divisions, the actual constellations associated with them vary in size, from huge Virgo (46°) to little Libra (18°). These irregular divisions are used by bio-dynamic calendars and differ from those used here for one-sixth of the time (some 60° in the circle of the zodiac).

Bio-dynamics developed within the anthroposophical movement founded by Rudolf Steiner which had drawn up its own 12-fold division of the heavens, loosely based upon the divisions made by the International Astronomical Union in 1928. The astronomers then decided to map out 13 constellations as lying on the ecliptic (Ophiucus, the Serpent-Bearer, being the thirteenth). The anthroposophists wanted no truck with this, however, and reconstructed a zodiac of just 12 constellations. Whereas the astronomers saw Libra as being 23° in length along the ecliptic, the anthroposophists gave it a mere 18°.

Sidereal and tropical zodiacs allocate equal spaces to each sign, but Steiner and his followers attempted to reflect astronomical reality more closely. The constellations by which they divided their calendar are therefore, by their very nature, unequal in size.

There was no great harm in any of this; indeed it was quite audacious. The trouble began when Maria Thun imposed the four elements on to this irregular set-up in the 1950s. Her use of these divisions made for a radical imbalance in the four elements. Root days (Earth) were assigned over 50 per cent more of the month than the Flower days (Air). The Air-constellation Libra is very short, while the Earth-constellation Virgo is two and a half times longer. The system was badly out of kilter, but nobody seemed to mind.

The Sidereal Zodiac

The present calendar uses the zodiac of the stars as the optimal reference that really works in an organic-growing set-up. Its basis is thus traditional, a framework tried and tested over millennia. The element rhythm of the star-zodiac is a simple thing, which is why plants respond to it. Just as investigation of lunar influence on plants is a recent phenomenon, so is the rediscovery of the sidereal zodiac in the West. Traditional gardening manuals have used the tropical zodiac without question, largely because it was the only one known to them. With the steady accumulation of evidence supporting the sidereal zodiac framework, the practice of lunar planting can now be established on a firm foundation.

The Rhythm of the Sun

We have lost our cosmos by coming out of our responsive connection with it, and this is our chief tragedy. What is our petty little love of nature – Nature! – compared to the ancient magnificient living with the cosmos and being honoured by the cosmos.

D. H. Lawrence

 or long-term planning in agriculture, there are two cycles that really count: an 18-year cycle of the Moon – of which more later – and the 11-year rhythm of the Sun, its sunspot cycle. If you look at a slice through an old tree trunk, you should be able to see how its rings become widest about every 11 years. The wider rings show increased tree growth. The beat to which trees, and a host of other living things, keep time is that of the changing level of solar activity, as indicated by the number of sunspots visible on the surface of the Sun. At the peak level of solar activity, the solar magnetic field, north and south of the ecliptic, flips over once per 11 years, creating a complete 22-year cycle. A maximum of sunspots then reflects this peak in magnetic turbulence. Both 11-year and 22-year cycles have an effect on the Earth.

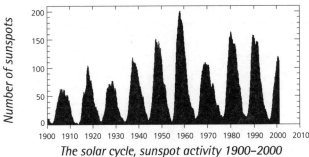

The solar cycle, sunspot activity 1900–2000

The Solar Rhythm in Agriculture

While lunar rhythms define optimal sowing days within one season, this grand pulse of the Sun determines the years of peak production – and also lean years. This expansion and contraction rhythm within the Sun affects rhythms of total crop production, and much else besides. Experts generally assume that this influence is an indirect one via the Sun's effect on climate: electrical and magnetic changes in the upper atmosphere around the Earth are caused by solar radiation, and these affect the climate, which in turn affects crop yield.

Ever since the astronomer William Herschel stated two centuries ago that the price of wheat varied with the sunspot cycle, scientists have been arguing as to whether the effect is really present. Meteorologists at the Appleton Laboratories in Slough, England, researched the subject, and their conclusions were quite positive. Led by Dr J.W. King, they found that in Britain root-crop yields of potato, turnip and swede tended to peak at years of sunspot maxima, and also that rainfall tended to increase during those years.

The scientists further found that the number of days per growing season (defined as days with a mean temperature above 6°C/43°F) increased markedly during years of peak activity. This confirms the observations of an English farmer Mr Farrar, reported in *Farmer's Weekly* in 1975, that the length of his cows' annual grazing season varied markedly with the sunspot cycle. Family records showed that his cows stayed out to graze longest in years of peak sunspot activity, presumably reflecting a longer growing period of the grass.

An effect on mean temperature over the sunspot cycle was also found for the US states Maryland, Delaware and Virginia (1900–60), which showed mean variations of 2–3°C/4–5°F linked with the solar rhythm – although this correlated primarily with the 22-year cycle rather than the 11-year cycle. This has relevance, Dr King argued, for energy budgeting as regards fuel consumption.

Can farmers expect bumper harvests in years of sunspot maxima and more meagre yields in years when the Sun is quiet? More research is needed on Sun–Earth links before such recommendations can be made, but it may not be long before farmers take account of this solar pulse when planning ahead.

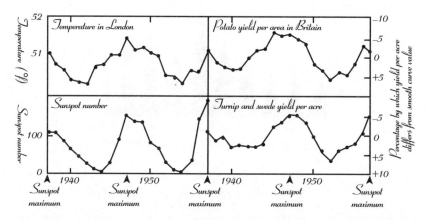

Variations in temperature, sunspot activity and yields of potatoes, turnips and swedes through two complete sunspot cycles (after King et al., 1974)

The effect of sunspot activity is also geographically dependent. Since most wheat is grown in the northern hemisphere and yields are increased in years of peak activity, global wheat prices tend to be lower at those times. King found modulations of 10–50 per cent in production in China, the US and the former Soviet Union. The solar cycle may be more evident in northern latitudes, where a greater flux of energised solar particles can funnel down into the atmosphere, as shown in the aurora borealis. In the southern hemisphere the cycle is reversed, with least growth in years of sunspot maxima. Dr King and others have suggested this as a basis for global economic planning.

Overall rainfall is also linked to the sunspot cycle. Dr R.G. Vines in Australia found that years of drought in certain countries are linked to troughs in the sunspot cycle, and also that large forest and prairie fires occur more often in these years. He counted bad fire-years as those on which losses overall due to fires were of one million acres or more. It is perhaps not surprising that fires on Earth should be linked to rhythms in the fiery energy of the Sun. Major US droughts seem to remain in step with the 22-year rather than the 11-year cycle.

Other phenomena have been shown to vary with the Sun's cycle. For example, years of peak activity seem to produce good wines. This appears both for French Burgundy and for German Rhine wines. The Russian expert Professor Alexsander Chizhevsky studied the relationship of the sunspot cycle to human history, claiming that more political upheavals, unrest and warfare took place in years of peak activity. Modern radio and electrical communication companies take a practical interest in the cycles of the Sun because they get more disturbance and interruption during times of solar storms.

When the Moon blots out the Sun during a total eclipse and the sky grows dark, the red rim of the solar chromosphere appears around the edge. This chromosphere, on years of sunspot maxima, will glow all around the Moon, whereas on quiet years of sunspot minima it is seen to glow each side of the Moon's black rim only at low solar latitudes. This means that, although normally invisible, the Sun's chromosphere expands and contracts over the 11-year cycle.

The Nutation Cycle

In the 1980s, reports started appearing of the 18.6-year lunar-node cycle present in climatic and agricultural records, and it is now viewed as being at least as influential as the solar pulse. Rainfall or drought is linked with this node or nutation cycle, in several parts of the world, for example the monsoons of India, tidal waves in the Earth's oceans, and the 19-year cycle in the flooding of the Nile.

The US cycles expert Dr Robert Currie has found that droughts in the US Midwest are caused by the 18.6-year node cycle. It affects atmospheric tides, which in turn influence the flow of rain-bearing air to the Midwest region. This area, where much of the world's grain is grown, is well known to suffer severe droughts about every 20 years. High-yield periods in the US, almost free of drought, tend to occur near minimum declination. The El Niño weather pattern, a global reverberation in climate affecting atmospheric perturbation, droughts and so on, also appears to be strongly linked to this nodal cycle.

Currie found that these cycles – 18.6 and 11 years – are both present in the atmosphere, the lunar signal being stronger than the solar. He has traced the 18.6-year cycle through floods and droughts in China for the past five centuries.

As with the sunspot cycle, half the cycle can often appear as the effective length. For example, the lunar declination, which relates to how high the Moon rises in the sky, varies with the 18.6-year nutation cycle; however, eclipses take 9.3 years, half the nutation cycle, to revolve around the seasons of the year, there being no difference between the north and south nodes in this regard. There is a 9.3-year cycle in US grain production and prices, with high corn yields occurring in years of minimum declination, while the lowest agricultural prices tended to occur every 18.6 years. Currie has also argued that a crop production cycle of 18.6 years exists. US pig, chicken and egg production also varies with the node cycle: 100,000,000 more chickens were produced in the US at the peak than the trough between 1910 and 1960 – the largest lunar influence yet identified. Herschel's original comment on corn prices and the rhythm of the Sun may therefore be adjusted to match more of a lunar than a solar rhythm.

The effects of these cycles has serious implications for global food production, and hopefully increased knowledge will lead to them being used in long-term agricultural and economic planning.

A Quiet Sun and Global Cooling

As of February 2013, the new sunspot maximum seems very lethargic. It's supposed to be peaking this year but so far solar experts have not seen much sign of it. This is the fifth year of this cycle 'number 24', and we've experienced five years of colder winters. The previous minimum of 2005–2006 saw some of the quietest solar weather ever. Some experts believe that the present weak solar maximum augurs a future era of global cooling. The solar expert Dr Theodor Landscheidt told me this years ago in relation to this decade and I could not believe him! The Sun is not putting out strong solar flares, its sunspot numbers are low, and the solar wind pressure is also low so don't hold your breath for any big sunspot maximum. For reading on this subject, I would recommend *Chill, a Reassessment of Global Warming Theory* by Peter Taylor, who was quite influenced by Dr Landscheidt.

The Moon and Crop Yield

To speake then of the outward and active knowledge which belongs to our English Hous-wife ... Shee shall also know the time of the yeere, moneth and Moone, in which all hearbes are to be sowne; and when they are in their best flourishing, that gathering all hearbes in their height of goodnesse, shee may have the prime use of the same ... In February in the new of the Moone shee may sow Spyke, Garlicke, Borage, Buglose, Chervyle, Coriander, Gourds, Cresses, Marjoram, Palma Christi, Flower-gentle, white Poppy, Purslan, Radish, Rocket, Rosemary, Sorrell, Double Marigolds and Time. The Moone full shee may sow Anisseedes musked, Violets, Bleets, Skyrrits, White Succory, Fennell and Parslie. The Moone old sow Holy Thystell, Cole Cabadge, white Cole, greene Cole, Cucumbers, Harts Horne, Diers Grayne, Cabadge, Lettice, Mellons, Onions, Parsnips, Larkes Heele, Burnet and Leekes.

Gervase Markham, *The English Hous-wife*, 1615

hereas the phase or synodic cycle is related to the general growth of a plant, it is the sidereal cycle that is mainly linked to the final crop yield. A sidereally based rhythm applies to one instant in a plant's life, when the seed is sown on moist ground and its growth begins. At this critical moment, when DNA starts to duplicate, it is the Moon's position against the zodiac that influences how the seed's potential will come to fruition.

Systematic investigation of how the time of sowing affects final growth really started with the experiments of Maria Thun in Germany in 1956 (*see also* page 13). This method had been followed in investigations in Steiner's anthroposophical society since the 1930s, but it was Thun who had the idea of picking out the element rhythm rather than the separate Moon–zodiac constellations.

One row of seeds was sown every few days, each time the Moon reached the middle of a new zodiac constellation, so that 12 rows were sown in the course of one revolution of the Moon around the zodiac, usually in May. Each of these rows was then allowed to grow for the same period of time and, after harvesting, the weights of the crops from each row were compared. Results for potatoes have been published since 1972 (co-authored with statistician Dr Hans Heinze) but other crops have been subjected to the same research.

Thun's research garden, located in a small, tranquil village surrounded by hills near Marberg in Germany, carries on this work. Over the decades she has developed a remarkable insight into the way in which cosmic influences affect crop yield. The dominant effect emerging from her trials related to a four-fold pattern in the zodiac, which allocates each of the 12 constellations to the four elements, as described on pages 10–11. For potatoes, maximum yields occurred in the three rows which were sown on Root days, when the Moon was in front of one of the three zodiac constellations traditionally associated with the Earth element, while minimum yields tended to occur when the Moon was standing in one of the Water constellations. The yield increases obtained were in the region of 30 per cent for the three Earth-element sowings as distinct from the other nine.

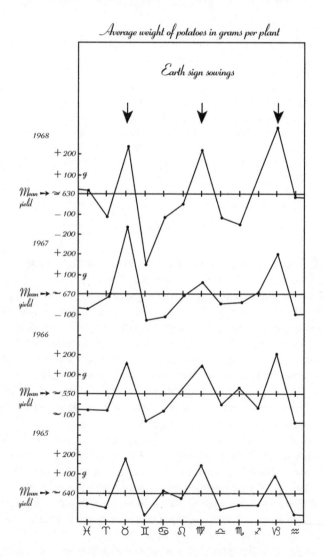

Potato yields according to the experiments of Maria Thun (1979)

Other studies using a similar experimental procedure have confirmed this four-element theory. Ulf Abele at Giessen University, as part of a doctoral study of bio-dynamic farming methods, tested barley, oats, carrots and radish during 1970–4, sowing 12 rows over the course of a month for each year. His barley and oats gave yields increased by 7 per cent overall when sowings were made on Fruit-seed (Fire) days, while his carrots and radish averaged a 21 per cent yield increase on the Root-day sowings (related to Earth).

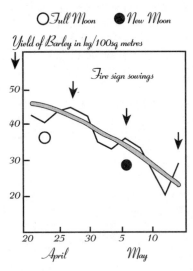

Barley yields according to Abele (1973)

A German study by Ursula Graf investigated the Moon–zodiac rhythm for different soils. Over the three years 1973–5, potato and radish crops were investigated and yield increases were usually found for Root-day sowings as the theory predicted. However, this occurred only in crops grown on organically cultivated soil to which no chemicals had been applied, and not in crops grown on soil treated with synthetic fertiliser. Graf's conclusion was, *The soil seems to be a decisive factor in the occurrence of connections between Moon–zodiac constellations and crop yields'*, a view which directly echoes Thun's comment in 1964:

'I came to the conclusion that mineralised soils hardly reacted to these cosmic rhythms and their fine influences, whereas a humus-filled soil of whatever soil type was a good mediator for these forces.'

In other words, only organic gardeners are going to reap important benefits from the calendar and method of working used here. Soil quality is very relevant to the way lunar influence will show up and may account for variations in results achieved.

In Britain in 1976, Reg Muntz, a market gardener in Sussex, planted 24 rows of potatoes over two sidereal months. The results showed a mean yield increase of 25 per cent for rows sown on Root days compared to other sowings. Other trials by Muntz, which I helped to design, involved beans, carrots and lettuce. Maximum yields consistently showed up in the element trigons, whereas there was little indication of a lunar-phase effect.

Some thorough experiments were done in Wales over three years by Colin Bishop, amateur gardener and astrologer. In 1976, he planted 36 rows of lettuce over three months and achieved the results shown below. The average weight of the lettuce tops increased by about 50 per cent for those rows sown on Water-element (Leaf) days when compared with sowings made on other days. A repeat of the experiment in 1977 produced substantially the same results. In 1978, Bishop experimented with daily sowings of radish and again found that the relevant days, in this case Root days, produced the highest yield by 45 per cent. None of these data-sets showed a Moon-phase effect on crop yields.

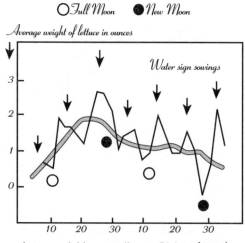

Lettuce yields according to Bishop (1976)

There is skill involved in growing rows of vegetables uniformly so that they aren't eaten by birds or slugs, and that lettuce form their hearts without bolting. Such uniform growth conditions are vital for the data to mean anything. Overall, in 1975–86, Muntz and Bishop grew some 400 rows of different vegetables in such trials and the net yield increase from sowing in the predicted trigons was 22 per cent. The soil used was not especially rich. The British results formed the groundwork for putting forward the calendar used here.

In 1980, J. Lücke sowed, as part of a doctoral thesis at the University of Giessen, four different plots of potatoes, with 12 rows per plot, one per Moon constellation. His Root-day yields were significantly in excess of the others, just as yields from the Leaf-day sowings were the least.

Sometimes a low-amplitude effect is observed, as in the extensive trials designed by Dr Hartmut Spiess. In three years of carrot trials 1979–81 at Dottenfelder farm near Frankfurt his yields averaged 8 per cent more on Root days, a small but significant increase as he undertook many sowings. The plot used was in an industrialised region of Germany where one might expect any sidereal-rhythm effects to be diluted. Some degree of scepticism has developed amongst bio-dynamic experts in Germany over the Thun model, focusing on the Spiess results as if they had failed to confirm the sidereal rhythms. I've gone into print arguing that they are low-amplitude effects and not null results. But let's agree with Spiess that:

'The magnitude of the yield deviations that were associated with lunar factors was of practical significance.'

For a practical, Australian view of how to use the sidereal rhythms we may quote from the lectures of Alex Podolinsky:

'The market gardeners may have noticed the best beans you have ever picked are on plants that are not huge and have not all that many leaves ... Now if you sow beans under a "leaf" zodiac sign, then they turn out such huge plants and they have very poor fruit. When you sow under a "seed" sign, you don't have all that much foliage (the plants don't need it, anyway) but they do have a lot of fruit. For pumpkins, in our experience, sowing under Leo is the most desirable ... We have run such trials and we have had roughly four times as many pumpkins in roughly the same acreage sowing them under Fruit rather than under Leaf.'

A Quality Test

Is the taste of a crop, as well as weight yield, affected by the trigons? Jack Temple, the well-known *Here's Health* organic-gardening correspondent, performed such a test in the spring of 1982, using the Thun sowing calendar:

'Every time a Leaf-sowing date turned up I sowed a row of lettuce and a row of radishes, and every time a Root-sowing day featured in her calendar we also sowed both lettuce and radish again. Then, when the directors and students from the Henry Doubleday Research Association dropped in on their yearly visit we put the trial to the test.'

Initially, Jack's visitors were shocked by this outlandish notion, so his reputation with them was at stake.

'However, all that disappeared as I put my knife through two radishes. One was juicy and the other had the texture of cotton wool. The juicy one had been sown on the correct day, a Root day, and the pithy radish had been sown on a Leaf day. That was not all: the juicy radish was ten weeks old while the pithy one was only eight weeks old. Both radishes were also tasted for quality and flavour.

Subsequently further sowings were tested. Each time we had the same result. Radishes sown on Leaf days were pithy and radishes sown on Root days were firm and fleshy. The lettuce trials did not produce quite such clear evidence, but lettuce sown on Leaf days were slower to bolt than those sown on Root days.'

To date, the evidence from such sowing trials demonstrates an effect caused by the primary element rhythms of the zodiac, but not for specific signs, as if plants, being simpler in their organisation than people, respond to this less-differentiated rhythm embodied in the zodiac. The weight of evidence to date indicates that the Thun model is valid and that the final yield of crops, when sown in good, organic soil, is related to the Moon's position according to the sidereal zodiac sign-element at the time of sowing.

The Lunar Nodes

There is at present less evidence for the effects of the lunar nodes on plants. According to Thun, the influence of the two nodes is liable to interfere with plant growth and to weaken the viability of seeds from plants sown at these times.

At perigee, when the Moon draws nearest to the Earth, the tides are pulled higher, rising some 30 per cent more than at apogee. It has been claimed that perigee is linked with stress. Thun has claimed that the apogee position causes sowings to sprout up rather quickly – which may not necessarily be beneficial for fruit formation – whereas the perigee position tends to inhibit growth. Evidence for the supposed adverse effect upon growth of perigee remains scant.

Sowing and Harvesting in the Phase Cycle

Does sowing at some point in the phase cycle produce better crops? Widespread folk traditions have suggested that it does. Modern experiments have been equivocal, though field experiments by Mather at the John Innes Horticultural Foundation in 1940 showed a consistent 15 per cent yield increase for maize and tomatoes sown on the second lunar quarter, confirming the hypothesis that the gardener had wished to test – the view that Kolisko had just published in *Agriculture of Tomorrow* (1939). Despite this confirmation, the author of the report was quite dismissive of his results. Crop-yield sowing trials that I've seen or been involved in have failed to detect much by way of any Moon-phase effects on crop yield. A comment by Thun on this issue is of interest:

'The influence of the Full Moon, throughout all the years of our research, only brought higher yields when these had been forced by mineral fertilisers or unrotted organic manures.'

Moonrise

A very thorough lunar-gardening experiment by Colin Bishop in 1978 used radish, sowing two rows in the morning and another two in the afternoon for over a month. The weight-yields did follow the star rhythm, peaking on Root days, but in addition there was a daily rhythm. The graph plots the Moon's motion against the horizon, centred on Moonrise. This graph was possible because Colin Bishop noted the time of each sowing, and also watered each row before inserting the seed – each morning on his way to work and then each afternoon as he returned. This means that the seed started growing as it was inserted into the soil. This is important if we are to take seriously the result: the hour of Moonrise showed up as the largest-amplitude effect in this data-set.

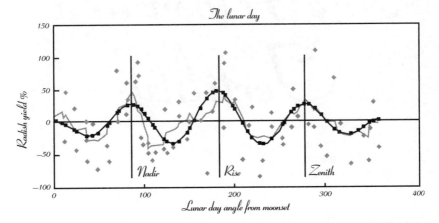

The lunar day, with Bishop's radish yields (1978)

There used to be a fine gardening column in *The Astrologer*, a London-based monthly of Victorian England, which always gave the time of Moonrise and recommended it be used for important gardening operations. Our calendar carries on this British tradition. My own opinion is that it is a very significant moment in the day when contemplating seed sowing or planting.

A New Year at Kew

Lunar-gardening research featured in the BBC2 programme *A New Year at Kew* in March 2007. Student Thea Pitcher of Kew's prestigious Royal Horticultural College had a plot allocated to her in 2006 for a research project of her choice. She decided to test this very book you are holding in your hand. Thea divided her plot into two, and sowed lettuce, sweet peas, onions, Swiss chard and leeks at 'right' and 'wrong' times.

On average, she told me, her lunar-planted vegetables showed about *30 per cent* more yield. It was an organic plot – Kew's Horticultural College favours organic methods whenever possible. Thea plans to write it all up for publication, and we may also see it featured on the website, www.plantingbythemoon.co.uk.

There was a BBC DVD available of all three series of *A New Year at Kew*, including the episode on Thea's work, which you may be able to find from second-hand sellers.

The Moon and Fertility

The thirteenth of the waxing month
Is a bad day to start seeding
But the best for transplanting.

Hesiod, *Works and Days*

 here seems little doubt that the lunar cycle influences the life processes of plants', wrote Dr Bernard Dixon, former editor of the *New Scientist*. Dr Dixon was referring to the Moon-phase cycle which affects many of the growth processes in a plant – metabolic rate, absorption of water and nutrients, rate of growth and electrical activity have all been observed to fluctuate in accordance with this rhythm. This is of enormous significance to farmers and gardeners.

The Phase Cycle and Plant Growth

The rate at which seeds germinate in relation to lunar phase was first studied systematically in the 1930s by Kolisko, who concluded that wheat germinated faster when sown at Full Moon than at New Moon. Confirmation of this result appeared in studies by M. Maw, funded by Canada's Department of Agriculture, on the rate at which cress germinated. Over a six-month period, batches of cress grown in water usually germinated quickest at Full Moon and slowest at New Moon, the difference in rate being very marked.

Traditionally, it has always been assumed that sap rose up into plants and trees maximally during the Full Moon. Therefore activities such as tree felling should be performed at New Moon, and crops would preserve best if harvested at New Moon, due to their minimal water content. While direct evidence from studies of sap in trees and shrubs is scant, a study by Professor Frank Brown and Carol Chow investigated day-to-day variations in the absorption of water by bean seeds under temperature-controlled conditions at their laboratory in North-western University, Illinois. Each day, the amount of water the seeds absorbed over a four-hour period was measured. Large maxima were found to occur just before the Full Moon, absorption being on average 35 per cent higher than at New Moon.

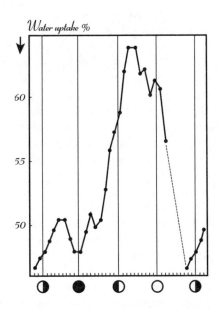

Water uptake by bean seeds (after Brown and Chow, 1973)

Biochemist Dr Harry Rounds at Wichita State University in the US reported that stress hormones in the blood of mice and men decreased sharply at Full and New Moon. He then extracted similar stress-related, 'cardio-acceleratory' substances from the leaves of various plants, especially geraniums, and found that their potency changed sharply for a short period following the Full and New Moon. His research is relevant to traditional advice that medicinal herbs should be picked at such times.

An important biochemical study was reported in 1989 from the University of Paris. It concerned a lunar pulse in plant DNA. Plant chromosomes, inside the nucleus of every cell, are large – much bigger than for animal cells. Two different types of structure were reported from x-ray studies. One, whose function is more related to storage of carbohydrates, was more developed at New Moon. Another type, more closely related to flowering and growth functions, was more developed at the Full Moon. This DNA response in plants is relevant to the traditional connection of the lunar cycle with fertility and growth.

A plant's metabolism can be assessed by how much oxygen it absorbs from the air. This was investigated in the classic experiments of Professor Frank Brown, in which potatoes and carrots were maintained in the dark over quite long periods, with the ambient conditions of temperature, humidity and pressure held constant. Through the years, he patiently charted over a million hours of potato time! From this, it emerged that the potatoes, although sealed from all light, were not at all in the dark about the cycles of the Sun and Moon. The Moon's daily rising and culmination (reaching its highest point in the sky) appeared as the hours of maximum metabolic rate for these root vegetables. In addition, their metabolic rate waxed and waned with the monthly lunar cycle: potato metabolism over the two weeks around the Full Moon was on average 15 per cent higher than that around the New Moon. For carrots the figure was 11 per cent.

A growing plant builds up an electrical field around it, in which the electrical potential at its top differs from that at the ground. This was investigated by Harold Burr, a professor at the Yale University School of Medicine. Burr decided to record the electrical potentials of trees by placing electrodes into their trunks. The first thing he discovered was that fluctuations in potential were the same for all the trees he investigated over a large area. Surprisingly, these were apparently unrelated to fluctuations in barometric pressure, humidity or the weather. He then monitored the potential of a single beech tree over a nine-year period, and this clearly showed that the dominant rhythm was tidal – 14.7 days – and that it peaked at the Full and New Moons. Analysis of this experiment showed that the tree's electrical activity was also responding to the level of solar activity (sunspots) but that the lunar cycles were stronger than these solar effects.

Bees are well adapted to the lunar month in their flight activity. Counters were fixed to beehive entrances by M. Oehmke, a biologist at the Goethe University, Frankfurt. Through the course of the year, these showed a huge lunar fluctuation in bee activity. This varied between species, one species being at least twice as busy at New Moon as at the Full. Bee activity fertilises flowers, reminding us of the connection between the synodic cycle and fertility.

Nowadays when we speak of a month we forget the lunar origin of this term, and do not consider the life-rhythms in all living things linked to this monthly cycle. No doubt humans, in our mechanical environment, respond less to the cycle of the month then other living things. *'On the days of the Full Moon, something colossal is taking place on Earth'*, averred Rudolf Steiner, in his agriculture lectures of 1924. He added the vital corollary, *'these forces spring up and shoot into all the growth of plants, but they are unable to do so unless rainy days have gone before.'* Plants, in spite of man-made changes, still live and grow attuned to this primary cosmic rhythm. These various results show that in plant growth, various different rhythms are related to the Moon's monthly cycle and that the time of Full Moon is especially important for them. Around this time a plant's metabolic rate and water absorption are at their greatest.

We have seen how laboratory studies indicate that a higher rate and speed of germination is attained if seeds are sown just before or round the Full Moon and, to a lesser degree, if sown over the New Moon; also that seeds and plants absorb water optimally around this part of the lunar month. In countries where drought is endemic this would have some bearing on the success of a crop and may have reinforced the idea that all plants should be sown around Full Moon.

Full Moon and Animal Husbandry

Geld hogs, steers, rams and kids when the Moon is waning.
Pliny, *History of Nature*

It seems that even nowadays many farmers who have never heard of Pliny's recommendations still follow them regarding castration and other surgery on animals, fearing complications due to excessive bleeding at Full Moon. There is some medical evidence to support this practice: some years ago a doctor in the United States investigated a group of 1,000 operations which had been performed in his hospital. He noted the Moon's phase at the time of all the operations in which complications from bleeding had occurred and found that at least four times more occurred at Full Moon than at New Moon. He analysed other groups of operations and obtained the same striking result. From this data, it appears that the period around the New Moon is indeed the optimal time for such operations, and that the Full Moon period should definitely be avoided. Animals also bite more at the Full Moon, or so the *British Medical Journal* reported in December 2000!

Horse Breeding

... [farmers] notice the aspects of the Moon, when at Full, in order to direct the copulation of their herds and flocks, and the setting of plants or sowing of seeds: and there is not an individual who considers these general precautions as impossible or unprofitable.

Ptolemy, *Tetrabiblos*, Ch. III

In the Middle Ages, the Arabs were the finest horse breeders in Europe and the Near East. Their subtle understanding of astrology may well have helped them in this breeding process.

Like cows, horses ovulate every three weeks throughout the breeding season. The vets can tell within a day or two if conception has occurred, therefore the record of mare coverings is a record of their times of ovulation. There is a tendency for horses to become synchronised in their ovulation, and hence for the stud farm to become more busy at three-week intervals. In this they resemble many

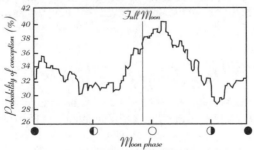

Horse fertility and the Moon

creatures in the wild, where the females tend to ovulate in synchrony. The diagram plots probability of conception at first covering around the lunar cycle (the data is smoothed with a 'moving average'). It clearly peaks on the days after Full Moon. Mare oestrus also tended to peak somewhere around Full Moon, being then in the region of 10 per cent more than at New Moon. In early 2005 my results on thoroughbred horse breeding and the lunar cycle, using 14 years of studfarm data, were published in *Biological Rhythm Research* (December 2004, 'Lunar Effect on Thoroughbred Mare Fertility', pp. 317–328). This clearly demonstrates, for the first time, the huge effect that the Full Moon exerts upon mare fertility and the modulation caused by the node cycle, which affects the strength of the Full Moon.

Harvest Time

Traditions link the time of harvesting crops to the Full or New Moons. One may believe that water and metabolic rhythms linked to this cycle should affect the final condition of a crop. Roman and Greek beliefs on this have already been touched upon. As an instance of modern awareness of lunar rhythms, here is the account of a Sydney-based company on the subject of their tomato harvest:

'We are growers of tomatoes, on a relatively large acreage, and found throughout the years that during the period of the Full Moon, a noticeable change takes place in the maturing and colouring of tomatoes. This quickening maturity, irrespective of temperature, only takes place two or three days before and after the Moon has reached its fullness.

During this period, marketplaces on the east and south coastal states have an influx of coloured fruit, where in normal times there is a high percentage of green and semi-coloured fruit. We have tested this out on many occasions and our statistics over many years have shown more fruit passing through our packing house through these periods, and that the fruit is much more forward in colour. These conclusions may well echo the experience of many growers.'

Such a clearly perceived effect reflects the more regular and predictable climate of Australia compared with Britain.

For crops that are to be dried, where juiciness and high water content are not required, at or just before New Moon seems the appropriate time for harvesting. Thus, the great French herbalist Maurice Messengé always picked his herbs at this time. He dried the herbs before use and believed that their virtue would preserve best if picked then.

Moonstamp for Timber

A related practice which can be traced back to antiquity is that of felling timber at the New Moon. The founder of the US Cycles Foundation in Pittsburgh described how in South America the Moon phase at which timber was felled was stamped on the wood, the idea being that New Moon timber preserves better and cuts more easily than that felled at Full Moon. French law from 1669 until the Revolution specifically required that timber be felled only during a waning Moon, a practice directly echoing the words of the Roman historian Plutarch:

'The Moon showeth her power most evidently in those bodies which have neither sense nor lively breath; for carpenters reject the timber of trees fallen in the Full-Moon as being soft and tender, subject also to the worm and putrefaction, and that quickly by means of excessive moisture.'

Accounts of this practice (discussed in Kolisko's *Agriculture of Tomorrow*) give the impression that the effect is more evident in tropical or sub-tropical regions. The experience of the Australian bio-dynamic farmer Alex Podolinsky is relevant:

'There is more water in trees and grass and all plants towards Full Moon than towards New Moon. In the old days, good timber cutters chopping down valuable timber would never cut other than towards the New Moon. They would not cut towards Full Moon, the timber was not as good. If we cut hay we also cut as much as possible towards New Moon and not towards Full Moon. We get much better quality hay that way.'

On the Trout Farm

It isn't just plants that have their fortnightly rhythms of growth. Trout in an aquarium grow to a rhythm whereby their weight peaks just before the Full and New positions. This was shown using several hundred small trout, and weighing them every four days – a commendably simple experiment.

Fish respond biochemically to the lunar cycle. Salmon and some species of trout hatch in fresh water and at a certain stage of their lives transform to become ocean-dwelling, salt-water fish. Salmon fisheries need to be able to predict this event as they have to release hatchery-reared fish into the river shortly before it occurs. The thyroid hormone thyroxine triggers this big moment in the salmon's life, and there is a specific New Moon in the spring which times this hormone surge. If the salmon wish to swim down the river without being seen by predators then a New Moon is the optimal time of month for them. This was discovered by zoologists at the University of California who concluded that a lunar calendar was essential for efficient culture of this economically valuable resource.

Back in the 1920s, an American called John Knight developed his theory about when to fish. He posited that fish feed only twice a day when the Moon either culminates (reaches its highest point) or reaches its nadir (lowest point below the horizon). For avid fishermen, the correct time to indulge their art can be calculated using our calendar. Six hours should be added to or subtracted from the given times of Moonrise. For the waning Moons, the calendar gives Moonset times, as they happen during the day

Gardening Aspects

To the better furthering of the gardener's travails, he ought afore to consider, that the Garden earth be apt and good, wel turned in with dung, at a due time of the year, in the increase of the Moon, she occupying an apt place in the Zodiack, in agreeable aspect of Saturn, and well-placed in the sight of heaven ... for otherwise his care and pains bestowed about the seeds and plants, nothing availeth the Garden.

Thomas Hill, *The Gardener's Labyrinth*, 1577

s viewed from the Earth at Full Moon, the Sun and the Moon are said to be in opposition. Two weeks later at New Moon they form the aspect called conjunction. An aspect is an angle, measured around the ecliptic from the centre of the Earth, expressing a symmetry within the zodiac. In order of decreasing strength, the aspects are:

conjunction (0°)

opposition (180°)

△ trine (120°)

□ square (90°)

✳ sextile (60°)

The square and opposition are considered inhibiting and stressful, whereas the trine and the sextile are thought to be beneficial and harmonious.

Each month, the Moon forms similar angles or aspects with Saturn and with the other planets. The Moon–Saturn relationship seems to have particular importance to agriculture and the life of plants. Our calendar indicates most of the Moon–Saturn aspects as they occur, some Moon–Sun aspects when they are relevant, and all the aspects between Moon and Venus as they fall on Flower days. The Venus aspects are recommended for working with flowers – sowing, planting out and grafting. In his ever-popular *Herbal*, Culpeper gave advice about when to pick herbs in terms of finding the right celestial aspects:

'Let them be full ripe when they are gathered, and forget not the celestial harmony before mentioned; for I have found from experience that their virtues are twice as great at such times as others.'

Aspects to Saturn

The planet Saturn was traditionally viewed as important for farmers. The Roman god Saturn presided over agriculture (his name is thought to derive from the Latin *sator*, sower), and the Saturnalia, held just before the winter solstice, was a week-long, lively agricultural festival in memory of the Golden Age. Indeed classical writers have mentioned no other planet in this regard. In his agricultural poem *Georgics*, Virgil advised, *'Watch the transit of the cold star Saturn.'* Saturn's sickle had a more rustic meaning before it came to denote the limitations of time. In astrological terms, Saturn represents life's challenging, defining and shaping principle. It is also sometimes depicted as Chronos, Old Father Time.

As an example of this traditional view, the sixteenth-century work on gardening lore, *The Gardener's Labyrinth*, explained about sextile aspects between Saturn and the Moon: *'it is then commended to labour the earth, sow, and plant'* whereas, during the square aspect between these two, it was *'denied utterly to deal in such matters.'* The trine was also approved, but the opposition was not.

Much the same advice featured in seventeenth-century British works, for example, *The Whole Art of Husbandry*, while *Dariotus Redivivus* advised that farmers:

'ought to have a special respect to the state and condition of Saturn, that he be not ... afflicted, because he hath chief dominion over husbandry and the commodities of the Earth; let him therefore (if you can so fit it) be in good aspect ... to the Moon.'

For planting crops, the general advice was: *'Plant what you intend, the Moon being either in conjunction, sextile or trine of Saturn.'*

Modern bio-dynamic farmers also consider the lunar opposition to Saturn to be important, so for some time it was the only celestial aspect to feature in their calendar. It is interesting to note that the Foundation for the Study of Cycles, based in Pittsburgh, USA, has found a 29.8-year cycle in famines, a frequency which corresponds almost exactly with the average time it takes Saturn to make one complete revolution through the zodiac.

Our calendar gives the lunar aspects of conjunction, opposition, trine and sextile to Saturn for Leaf, Flower and Fruit-seed days, but not for Root days, as there would be little point in sowing trees and perennial crops on Root days. The harmonious times – trine and sextile – are suitable for sowing perennials and trees, through Saturn's association with long-term cycles, and for increasing the hardiness of plants. Stressful times – conjunction, opposition and square – should be avoided. However, readers may wish to test the belief of bio-dynamic farmers that the opposition is the best Saturn aspect to use.

All aspects are given to the nearest ten minutes GMT. The best time to sow or plant is between one hour before and half an hour after the aspect occurs, although if that is impossible for practical reasons, sow within six hours before, rather than after the event.

Vines and the Sun

Readers with a warm and sunny spot in the garden may wish to try growing vines. For the ancients and for traditional astrological-rustic books, the vine had a solar rulership. The US biologist-astrologer Lee Lehman compared rulerships of all sorts of plants from a variety of traditional sources and she found a nucleus for which all her sources agreed. The vine was one of these. Most of these don't concern us, as planetary events are not given in the calendar (it would be too complicated). However, the main Sun–Moon aspects are given and these are the important options for when to establish a vine, particularly cutting the scion in autumn and grafting it in spring. These tasks should also be done on a Fruit-seed day.

The ancients also related wine quality to the movement of Jupiter around the zodiac. As it orbits once in 12 years, it enters a new zodiac sign each year. Various astrologers I consulted expressed surprise about the solar rulership of the vine, as they had expected it to be ruled by Jupiter. All those words associated with jovial derive from that sphere in the sky: Jupiter, or Jove. Those seriously considering setting up a vineyard might also research solar aspects to Jupiter or Venus.

To help understand this idea, let's quote from a recent book on plant rulerships by Jean Elliott which brought Culpeper's *Herbal* up to date. She gave the grapevine as solar in its rulership and summarised solar qualities as follows:

'The Sun: *Core essence, integrated conscious self, playful self, vitality. Play, children; palaces and mansions; day; gold. The Sun rules Leo. Colour: yellow, orange, gold.'*

Its section on plants ruled by the Sun reads:

'Grapevine: (Vitis vinifera). *Lilly, Culpeper [referring here to two seventeenth-century astrologers who gave rulerships]. Either grows as a long-lived climber or in bush form for wine. Green/white flowers from early to midsummer. Grapes in Autumn. Under 'Vine' in* Herbal. *Brought to Britain by the Romans.'*

Eighteen years ago, one of the most respected French wine estates, Clos de la Coulée de Serrant in Savennières, owned by Nicholas Joly, changed over to bio-dynamic principles. Under azure skies in the Loire valley, there are two wines now produced using a lunar calendar: Joly's and Noel Pinguit's Le Haut Lieu. The latter has won every award going (described as 'a stunningly intense, joyful wine' – solar qualities, perhaps). One per cent of French wine is currently produced according to a bio-dynamic regime. Joly expresses his views in rather solar terms:

'When we look at a flower or fruit, it becomes perfectly clear that they owe their beauty, their colour, their fragrance, their variety of shapes and flavours to the Sun. And it is precisely this power of expression, which manifests itself in constantly new variations, that must again be allowed to flourish again in wine – and in every foodstuff.'

As the grapes ripen, a critical situation develops in the last few weeks, crucial for final quality as the grapes have to be collected at optimal ripeness. As acidity gradually decreases, the sugar content rises. After harvesting, they are crushed and the mix poured into barrels. That moment needs careful choosing, being the 'birth-moment' of what will mature into wine, so make sure it's a Fruit day.

Maria Thun is collaborating with a wine-grower in the South of France. When I went to visit, her research plot of vines was being treated with various sprays of different copper concentrations. Copper sulphate is regularly sprayed on to vines as an insecticide, but she was using much weaker concentrations along the lines of homoeopathic medicines, to investigate their efficacy against infestation.

The year 1990 was a sunspot maximum, and is regarded as a classic wine year. The last maximum occurred in 2001. As the Sun expands, with solar flares extending further out from its surface and aurorae maximising at Earth's poles, are the best wines then formed? To quote from Gauquelin's classic, *The Cosmic Clocks*:

'According to the French Astronomical Bulletin, years in which the number of Sun spots is highest are great vintage years for Burgundy wines; in years with few Sun spots poor vintages are produced. The Swiss statistician A. Rima found similar results when he analysed the production of Rhine wines for the past 200 years.'

The Malignity of a Solar Eclipse

The great astronomer Johannes Kepler composed calendars that prognosticated for the year ahead and in one of them (1602) he explained how it all worked. He described an early version of the Gaia theory, whereby the Earth had a vegetable-animal force which had a sense of geometry, which enabled it to respond to the celestial aspects in terms of climate, harvests, good wine years and political stability. Kepler gave an analogy to explain how this worked: just as a peasant could take delight in the piping of a flute without knowing anything about the theory of musical harmony, so the Earth could respond in an unconscious way to the changing geometry of the heavens. The Earth more or less shuddered during an eclipse, he wrote:

'Eclipses ... are so important as omens because the sudden animal faculty of the Earth is violently disturbed by the sudden intermission of light, experiencing something like emotion and persisting in it for some time.'

Early tablets from ancient Babylon testified to the belief in the infertility of the land around the time of an eclipse. As a belief, it has endured longer than most. The early bio-dynamic sowing calendars by Franz Rulni advocated not sowing anything important for several days after an eclipse, while its successor, the modern Thun calendar, gives just the day of an eclipse as not good for planting.

In the Netherlands, there is a garden with a few ragged pear trees which only started to bear small, bitter fruit nine years after they were planted. As a test, they were deliberately planted at the inauspicious moment of a solar eclipse by Karen Hamaker-Zontag, the eminent Dutch astrologer. It would be interesting to see more tests done on this phenomenon.

That eclipses do diminish seed quality was demonstrated a few decades ago in a series of seed-germination experiments by Theodor Schwenck, which are summarised in his classic work, *Sensitive Chaos*.

The Organic Way

Clear the sheds of dung, but not at new moon or half moon.

Cato, *On Farming*

he sidereal rhythms described in this book will work optimally for the gardener using organic methods. An interest in lunar gardening goes hand in hand with organic growing. Organic soil can produce crops healthy enough to respond well to these cycles, whereas soil that has been chemically fertilised may not, or not to the same extent. Organic soil is built up over the years to be humus-rich with compost and well-rotted manure. If inorganic fertilisers are relied upon, on the other hand, these will force the growth of plants, initially increasing quantity but not quality, and decreasing storage life, disease resistance and soil quality.

Organic farming has been defined as growing crops free from herbicides, pesticides, fungicides and inorganic fertilisers. At one stage, organic growing was considered the province of cranks, but all that has changed, with a broader view of organic production as working in harmony with, rather than in opposition to, nature. With huge food surpluses from overproduction and farmers being paid to set aside productive land, it is an advantage that the organic way involves a slower rate of growth and a lower final crop yield, relying on natural rhythms and quality. While organic growing tends to be more labour-intensive, this can also be seen as a movement towards a community of workers. Working with the seasons is another advantage, as produce always tastes best when harvested and eaten at the right time.

A five-year study published by the US Department of Agriculture found that organic farms had yields roughly equal to, and costs considerably lower than, conventional farms. Organic farms used more labour per unit of produce, but consumed less energy. Panels of tasters tend to prefer organic food, and organic foods tend to have a longer shelf-life. The concept of quality is being refined by these and other investigations and should be of great relevance for future studies of lunar influence. We are moving towards a positive definition of what 'organic' means in terms of taste and other characteristics, and not merely the absence of chemical products.

The organic way also has advantages where livestock are concerned. Research in animal husbandry has confirmed that animals fed on organic diets are more fertile and less prone to disease. With human male fertility apparently continuing a long-established downtrend, this may have even broader implications. In the 1990s epidemic, no cows born and bred on organic farms got BSE. Indeed, bio-dynamic farms received a boost when a statement made in 1923 by Rudolf Steiner was unearthed: if cows were fed on meat produce, he said, they would go mad.

The Organic Market

The organic movement really took off during the 1980s, largely as a northern and middle-European phenomenon. There are 4,000 registered organic producers in the UK. Demand continues to grow at a phenomenal rate – organic sales had increased to £1.12 billion in 2003–2004. About 10 per cent of farmland in Austria, Denmark and Sweden is organic, while the figure is around 2 per cent in Germany, France, Italy and the UK. Almost 10 per cent of British organic farms are bio-dynamic and there are now about 50 such farms. Many organic farms are offering delivery services or supply through local farmers' markets, in order to allow more consumers to access their products, ensure seasonal produce and minimise transport of goods.

In 1993, an EU regulation laid down a legally binding standard of guidelines for organic farming which sufficed to block US legislation of 1998, permitting genetically modified, additive-treated and irradiated food to be sold as organic. The arrival of these new technologies poses rather urgently the question whether any kind of life-energy exists in food. Those with an interest in organic farming or lunar gardening must surely believe that it does.

Jack's Organic Garden

Jack Temple used to write the organic gardening section for *Here's Health* magazine and his columns were collated in his book, *Gardening without Chemicals*, which contained fascinating information about his gardening methods. He would also assure readers that sowing by the correct Moon element made a big difference, even for cress grown indoors: it was worth waiting a few days until the Leaf days came round, he reckoned, even if it meant storing the cress in the fridge for a while.

Jack was also an advocate of the organic principle. He would put calcified seaweed into his compost preparations, and also rock phosphate (from Chile). This is an inorganic chemical, but on the Soil Association's approved list because it is slow-release. Indeed, some gardeners don't like using it on the grounds that it is too insoluble.

After harvesting a vegetable plot, Jack wouldn't dig. He'd spread organic kitchen waste across the ground, with any vegetables the local shops were throwing out, then cut grass and nettles and a dusting of calcified seaweed. Then it was all covered with flattened cardboard boxes, and finally the plot was covered with black plastic sheeting to prevent weeds growing. Insects munched their way through beneath this, until in the spring the soil was friable and ready for the next crop. The taste of his vegetables was an experience.

The way he dealt with pests was also natural. There was an irrigation stream around his plot, which provided enough frogs to control the slugs. Once, a row of his beans was infested by blackfly. 'Needs some more compost,' Jack remarked. He was proud of his worm-compost. What connection compost application was supposed to have with blackfly infestation was far from clear to me, but it was applied and the next week, the blackfly were gone. He seemed to have the right attitude towards harnessing the forces of nature to human ends: ingenious, yet with proper respect.

Foot-and-Mouth Epidemic

In the last week of February 2001, the world's worst foot-and-mouth epidemic hit the headlines just as Saturn was coming into conjunction with Algol (at 26° of Taurus), which has the reputation of being the most evil star in the firmament, while Saturn is traditionally associated with agriculture. Saturn remained within one degree of Algol throughout most of March, as the British farming industry saw the progress of the massive extermination project directed by computer projections in London, rather than the advice of recognised foot-and-mouth experts who were advocating a different course of action. Meanwhile, an outbreak in the Netherlands was coped with, swiftly and with few deaths, by inoculation.

It is interesting to note that both Saturn and Jupiter were then in the Taurus constellation. They were separating, having been conjunct the previous year. While only a tiny proportion of the cows slaughtered were actually diagnosed as having the disease, it is significant that hardly any organically reared cows were diagnosed from the foot-and-mouth outbreak, just as not one cow born and bred as organic suffered from BSE.

Monthly Tasks in the Vegetable Garden

... the powerful grace that lies
In herbs, plants, stones, and their true qualities.

Friar Lawrence, *Romeo and Juliet*, Act II

Ken Whyatt, who has spent many years using organic methods, has kindly provided this excellent and practical seasonal guide to organic vegetable gardening throughout the year. I hope it will prove useful to the reader, even though climates may not be quite the same as for Ken in south-west England. While this guide gives valuable advice on when to carry out tasks throughout the year, readers will need to refer to the calendar for day-to-day information on when best to sow, tend and harvest particular crops.

January

Burn woody rubbish in a slow, smother fire. Sieve the resultant ash and mix it with an equal quantity of leaf mould to make a wonderful base for sowing seeds later on. Keep the ash in a dry place. Stack clods of earth round the bonfire; these will crumble and make a useful ingredient in a potting mixture for tomatoes later in the spring.

Spread compost on vacant land to remain until the soil is suitable for making seed beds.

Inspect all vegetables in store and safeguard against hard frosts by covering with straw, matting or other light, dry material.

Make a cropping plan for your plot, making sure that cabbages (and members of the cabbage family) and potatoes are rotated by planting them in an area not occupied by these crops for at least two years.

Order your seeds in good time. Early potato seeds should be chitted – placed in trays in a light, frost-free place so that they develop short green shoots – thus gaining several weeks' growth at planting time.

If your soil is a sticky clay, do not walk on the garden unnecessarily unless it is frozen. Keep a supply of old planks to put down to walk on when you pick sprouts and other winter crops in wet weather. This will ensure that your soil will be easier to dig in the spring.

If you have a sheltered area facing south and the soil is well drained and crumbly, make some sowings of early peas and broad beans (long-pod varieties). Cloches will give added protection.

You can also plant shallots if the soil is not sticky.

February

Lightly fork over the area intended for sowings of early carrots, lettuce, cabbage, beetroot (red beet) and parsnips. Incorporate well-rotted compost or leaf mould and sieved bonfire ash in the top 5 cm/2 in. If the soil is too sticky to rake to a fine tilth, keep it covered with cloches for a week or so.

Make small sowings of early peas, short-horn carrots, lettuce, summer cabbage and Brussels sprouts.

Delay sowings of parsnips and beetroot (Boltardy is recommended) until late in the month and choose a sheltered spot. Even then, beet will require the protection of cloches. These seeds are large and can be spaced about 5 cm/2 in apart. A small sowing should provide salad beetroot in June.

Parsnips should be sown at intervals of about 23 cm/9 in, in rows 45 cm/18 in apart. Seed must be fresh and it is advisable to sow in groups of three or four seeds to ensure even germination, the weaker plants being thinned out in April. To ensure the rows are well marked (parsnips are slow starters), sow radish about 2.5 cm/1 in apart in the same rows. These will be ready for pulling long before the parsnips have grown large.

Jerusalem artichokes can be planted about 30 cm/12 in apart. Remember they can attain a height of almost 2 m/6 ft so they can be used as a wind break, as shade for late sowings of lettuce and as an excellent vegetable in their own right.

Make your main sowings of broad beans this month. It is worth planning to succeed broad beans by a crop that requires plenty of nitrogen, such as cauliflower, autumn cabbage or broccoli. The beans' roots increase the soil's nitrogen content. When the crop has been picked, cut the top growth to ground level and leave the roots where they are.

March

A busy month if the weather is reasonable. It is better to wait until the end of the month before sowing than to sow on pasty soil. Broad beans are a worthwhile crop, but must be given plenty of room to develop. Pinch off the top 15 cm/6 in when they are in flower – the shoots make a delicious salad or cooked vegetable and the plants are less liable to attack from blackfly.

Sow main-crop Brussels sprouts, cabbages and short-horn carrots for summer use; celery or celeriac and leeks in seed boxes in garden frames or greenhouses.

Plant out lettuces from February sowings, ensuring they have plenty of compost in drills directly under their roots. Further sowings of lettuce should be made from now throughout the spring and summer. A pinch of seed will sow a short row of about 1.2 m/4 ft and this will suffice if sowings are made fortnightly. The same rule applies to radish, which are large seeds and can be dropped in a drill singly about 2.5 cm/1 in apart.

Buy onions as sets – onions whose growth has been arrested in the autumn – and plant them in fine soil manured for a previous crop. Just push them into the soil without bruising them, and cover their necks. As they start to root, they may push themselves out of the soil. Replant them with the tip of a trowel.

Parsnips can still be sown, but should be in by the end of the month if they are to attain maximum growth.

Peas can be sown in continuation. The taller kinds will need the support of twigs or netting and the rows should be far enough apart to make picking easy. Rows of lettuce or radish can be sown as catch crops between the peas at the same time, as these will mature before the peas are ready and will benefit from some shade.

Fine soil with plenty of compost is needed for a good yield of early potatoes. If these have two or three green shoots already formed (see January) they can be planted towards the end of March.

Spinach, spinach-beet and Swiss chard can now be sown, the last being the most useful, its thick, fleshy mid-ribs making a separate dish from the large, spinach-like leaves.

Annual weeds, and even perennial ones, will wilt in the sun if the surface of the ground is hoed slightly. They may look unsightly for a while, but worms will assist in clearing them, and the dying material will act as mulch.

Continue to plant out Brussels sprouts, cabbages, savoys and broccoli. There is still time to plant marrows and cucumbers outdoors if plenty of humus is available to give them a good start.

Plant leeks from seed beds. Trim about 2.5 cm/1 in off the leaf tips and trim back straggly roots, then drop them into holes made by a dibber about 20 cm/8 in apart and water in without pressing back the soil.

Runner beans and tomatoes will require strong stakes, which are easier to push in if the ground is soaked first. Plant after the stakes are in position.

April

Tomatoes can be sown in late March, but plenty of light and an average temperature of 15–18ºC/60–65ºF is necessary for a good start, so early April is usually better. Minimum requirements are a warm window-sill not subject to draughts, a good seed compost in boxes of 5-cm/2-in depth and thin sowing. When the seedlings are about 5 cm/2 in high they should be planted in separate 9-cm/3½-in pots and grown until early May in a warm, light place before moving to a cold greenhouse. Do not plant outdoors until late May or early June.

A useful plant is land or American cress, similar in appearance, taste and food value to watercress. Sow in a damp spot such as the north side of a low wall, or close to a concrete path, where it is easy to keep them watered.

The main sowings of dwarf beans, beet, broccoli, spinach, autumn and winter cabbages, carrots and herbs of various kinds can be made this month (bearing in mind that dwarf beans are frost-tender, so these could be delayed to late April or even May). January King cabbage and the varieties of purple and white broccoli are useful winter vegetables which will withstand hard frosts when greens are so expensive to buy. Incidentally, broccoli and Brussels sprouts need an open situation and at least 60 cm/2 ft between plants, with a good firm soil. Wind tends to rock them, so draw up some surrounding soil from time to time to hold their stems firm.

Early and maincrop potatoes should be planted before the end of the month, giving the maincrops a minimum gap of 60 cm/2 ft in the rows and 75 cm/2½ ft between the rows. If the early potatoes have come through the soil, earth them up slightly and cover with soil if frost threatens. Periodically, they should be earthed up, leaving a curved rather than a sharp ridge.

May

Take the opportunity during dull, showery weather to plant out seedling cabbages, cauliflowers and Brussels sprouts. Plant to the base of the lowest leaf stalks and make the soil really firm.

Plant out thinnings of lettuces but ensure the roots are not damaged. They must be thoroughly watered unless the weather is showery, and prefer a spot with some daytime shade.

Runner beans, courgettes, marrows and ridge cucumber are all sown this month, but must have some protection from late frosts. Cloches are ideal for this and home-made polythene frames or tunnels ensure a good start. Close up the ends with a sheet of glass, as wind-tunnels are not appreciated by any plant.

Early May is the best time for sowing maincrop beetroot, the thinnings of earlier sowings being useful raw in salads. Pick them when they are the size of a golf ball.

Late broccoli, savoys and winter cabbage, such as the excellent January King, are sown this month. Swedes and turnips are useful as a winter crop and should be thinned to 20 cm/8 in apart when 2.5 cm/1 in high.

Capsicums sown in the middle of May, given sufficient warmth, will provide green pods in the autumn.

It's not too late to sow carrots; in fact, the later sowings are less prone to attack from carrot fly. Incidentally, when thinning carrots for salads, remove the tops to the compost heap and tread back the soil loosened in the rows. The fly is attracted by the smell of carrots and likes to lay its eggs in loose soil.

Keep cauliflowers well watered with diluted liquid manure; they are the hungriest and thirstiest of plants, although celery must run them very close. Celery is naturally a ditch plant and does well in a trench with soil banked on either side. These ridges are useful for catch crops of lettuce or radish; when they have been gathered, the soil is used for successive earthing up of the celery for obtaining well-blanched stems.

Sweetcorn needs a sheltered, moist spot. Sow the seed to fill a square area rather than in rows. This assists pollination.

Peas can still be sown, but it's a good plan to leave the finished seed bed, after raking it over, at least 5 cm/2 in below the surrounding soil. You can then give them plenty of water.

In the third week, harden off tomato plants for outdoors. An improvised polythene-covered frame will suffice until the plants are put in their final positions early in June.

June

Dwarf and runner beans can be sown for a continuation of supply or if previous sowings have failed.

Lettuces will bolt if planted out in sunny positions. It is far better to sow thinly and then thin out, using any thinnings for salads. Afternoon shade provided by taller plants will lengthen the growing season.

Water will be required by most vegetables if rainfall is light; if it has been standing in tanks, so much the better. Always give a thorough watering; the effect of dribbles is to bring roots to the surface, only to be left high and dry. An all-night drenching from a sprinkler hose will do wonders to beans, lettuce, beet, celery and cauliflowers during a dry spell. In fact, plants benefit from evening soakings far more than any in the morning; the morning is a good time to add a mulch of lawn mowings before the sun can bake the surface of the soil. Mowings will gradually disappear as earth worms take them down, thus helping to aerate the soil and increase its fertility.

July

Complete planting of cabbages, savoys, Brussels sprouts, broccoli and leeks.

Swedes and hardy turnips can still be sown in the south of England or similar climates.

Spinach-beet and Swiss chard can be sown for next spring cropping.

Repeatedly pinch out side shoots from tomatoes, except bush varieties.

Harvest shallots and onions as they ripen and keep runner and dwarf beans picked as soon as they are large enough. Beans must never be allowed to grow coarse or they'll become unproductive.

Sow winter radish and thin to 15 cm/6 in apart.

A sowing of parsley in a sheltered spot should withstand the winter.

Dig early potatoes if ready. Keep the soil moist, remembering that showery weather is usually a good time to give a crop a soaking.

As plots become vacant, for example after onions have been harvested, it is a good plan to dig the soil, incorporating leafy vegetable rubbish and compost in shallow trenches as the digging proceeds across the plot. Woody waste such as cabbage stems are best disposed of on a bonfire, the plant ash being collected and kept in a dry place.

A sowing of a suitable variety of spring cabbage can be made in northern districts during the last week of July. In warmer areas, this is best deferred until the first week in August. Care in selection of a variety suitable to the district is advisable, as this is such a valuable crop.

Cucumbers, marrows and beans will benefit from good soakings of rain water that has been warmed by the sun. An excellent liquid manure can be made by chopping nettles or comfrey into rain-storage tanks and allowing them to soak for a few days. Tomatoes, in particular, benefit from this liquid, supplemented by a dressing of wood ash round the roots and followed by a mulch of lawn mowings. The plants will make rapid growth and set their trusses of fruit early.

August

The soil may now be rather dry for sowing seeds, and it's not advisable to water seeds after they are sown. You can overcome this by drawing a drill slightly deeper than normal, soaking this and sowing on top, then covering the seeds with fine sifted soil mixed with leaf mould or peat. The dry layer above the seeds will prevent rapid evaporation, keeping the seeds moist enough for quick germination. This method works well with seeds sown in August, such as onions, lettuce, winter radish and spring cabbage. If drought conditions prevail, a soaking from a fine sprinkler or a can with a fine rose can be followed with a light covering of hedge trimmings. These will soon wilt, but will prevent caking of the surface. Alternatively, you can use cloches after the watering, the cloches being lightly covered with hay or prunings for a day.

From spring until autumn, grass mowings not required for mulching should be rotted down on a compost heap. Layers of grass, not more than 5–7.5 cm/2–3 in thick, should be interspersed with garden and kitchen waste. Rotting will be faster if smaller quantities of animal manure are spread between layers and a dusting of lime is added from time to time. Good composting is quite an art, but there is no finer material obtainable for plant feeding than a well-rotted compost. Spread as a mulch between crops or on vacant plots as a weed smother. Worms will be active in the autumn, incorporating this material into the surface soil far more effectively than the gardener can ever do by digging it in.

Pick cobs of sweetcorn while still green.

Harvest onions as soon as the tops have died down.

Continue to pick tomatoes and beans as soon as they are ready. Surplus beans freeze well.

September

Plant out winter lettuce in land manured for a previous crop. On heavy soil it is advisable to plant on top of a slight ridge to avoid damping off. You can also make a further sowing of a winter-hardy variety.

Continue to lift potatoes and main-crop carrots. Store sound roots for future use. Do not leave these vegetables in the ground when they have reached their maximum growth, as slugs and other pests can do much damage.

September can be the worst month for weeds, many of which are hurrying to ripen their seeds for the autumn winds to scatter. Remove them to the compost heap where the warmth generated by lawn mowings should destroy them.

Vacant plots can be utilised by filling (but not overcrowding) them with cabbage, winter lettuce and spinach plants.

In dry spells, celery can be earthed up 5 cm/2 in at a time. The stems will then be blanched.

Use parsley as required from the seedling rows, leaving strong plants standing about 15 cm/6 in apart. Cover them with cloches if the plot is exposed to cold winds in the winter.

If your garden is exposed, or in a frost-pocket, it is as well to prepare for a slight frost towards the end of the month. The risk is greatest during clear anti-cyclonic weather when the morning sun does the damage. Polythene sheets or even newspaper draped over tomatoes and peppers will help to protect them and can be removed after an hour or so.

Gather ripened marrows for storage in a dry place.

Sow lamb's lettuce or corn salad. This is an invaluable salad which can be used during the early spring when lettuces are scarce and expensive. Cut like spinach.

October

Continue to pick tomatoes as they ripen and, if frosts are imminent, remove whole trusses of fruit to ripen in trays lined with newspaper. They will ripen in the dark providing they have warmth. The whole plants can be lifted, complete with roots, and hung in a cool greenhouse for the remaining fruits to ripen or be used green for chutney. With some care, it is possible to have ripened tomatoes until Christmas.

Dig the remainder of main-crop potatoes; they are liable to slug infestation if left in the soil. Ensure that the minute, undeveloped potatoes are removed, otherwise these can grow next year, possibly spreading disease to both tomatoes and potatoes.

Dig parsnips as required, although they will improve if frosted and can safely remain in the soil until you need them. Beetroot and carrots will not withstand hard frosts and are better stored in dry sand or peat in a cool place.

Put annual weeds on the compost heap. Put tree leaves in a separate heap as they take much longer to rot. Keep the garden tidy, removing yellowing leaves of the cabbage family and other decaying matter which only harbours slugs and other pests in the garden and is far better on the compost heap. Heavy land should be rough dug during the autumn and given a good dressing of compost. Light soil is best composted in the spring.

Spring cabbages are planted this month. If two varieties have been sown, so much the better. They should be firmly planted, closer than other cabbages, say 30 cm/12 in apart in rows 60 cm/2 ft apart. In spring, cut alternate cabbages, leaving the others to grow larger.

A final sowing of winter-hardy lettuce can be made early in the month, covering with cloches.

Celery should be earthed up during dry spells and celeriac lifted as required, the remaining roots being covered with dry soil to protect from hard frosts.

November

Clear up fallen leaves and put in a heap. Chicken netting will prevent them blowing about and the resulting leaf mould can be used at the bottom of next year's potato drills.

It is a good plan to turn semi-rotten compost, placing the outside to the middle and the middle to the outside of the new heap. When completed, give a sloping finish, dust with garden lime and cover with old matting to keep off excessive rain.

Woody waste, potato and tomato stems and diseased plants should be burnt in a slow, smother fire, if possible covered with clods. The ash and burnt soil can be sieved when cool, kept dry and used in sowing composts next spring.

Continue forking over vacant land and burning perennial weed roots. Leave the surface rough, or cover heavy land with rotted compost. A light forking is all that will then be necessary in the spring to prepare the soil for planting and sowing.

Jerusalem artichokes can be used as required and some stored in sand for use during hard frosts. Clear out all roots as they are dug. Even small pieces will grow next year and can become invasive. If you grow horseradish, the same advice applies.

On dry soils, a sowing of broad beans will repay the effort by producing a finer crop than those sown in the spring. If land is in danger of becoming too wet, the roots will rot so use cloches to help prevent this.

Corn salad or lamb's lettuce thrives in a dry, sheltered spot and is most useful in early spring salads. Sown early this month under cloches it should provide plenty of tender green stuff in April.

December

It is better to dispose of soft vegetable waste in winter by digging it into trenches during the rough digging of vacant plots than to put it on the compost heap where vermin may be a problem.

Plan ahead for the coming year, making a list of crops which bear well on your soil and ensuring that they will be planted in proper rotation. Leaf vegetables do well on soil previously used for bean crops because of the latter's nitrogenous deposits created by bacteria from nitrogen in the air. Potatoes, if well manured, provide a well-dug soil suitable for beans and peas the following year. Root crops can follow on after members of the cabbage family – give a scattering of lime before sowing; but keep lime away from land required for potatoes, otherwise the potatoes will have scabby skins.

In a four-year crop rotation of this sort, lettuce, tomatoes, celery, leeks and onions can be fitted in where they are likely to do best; but it is advisable to move onions and leeks around from year to year.

How to Use the Lunar Calendar

When you cut down elm, pine, walnut and all other timber, cut it when the Moon is waning, in the afternoon, and not under a south wind.

Cato, *On Farming*

 his calendar is designed as a practical tool for the gardener and farmer, containing the key information needed on the two monthly cycles for which there is substantial evidence of their effects on gardening: the waxing and waning Moon, and the sidereal 27-day cycle. It also includes other, less well documented but potentially important information about aspects.

Readers may wish to do their own research, sowing some of their crop at an optimal time and more at a negative time to see whether there is any difference in the results. Ideally, a proper experiment requires at least a dozen rows, with equal amounts of seed sown per row on different days, and all harvested in rotation after the same length of time. Over time, one can distinguish lunar patterns from effects created by weather or other influences.

It is not always easy to co-ordinate a gardening schedule to the Moon – we all seem to be so busy these days – but with a little planning it can be achieved, hopefully with a positive effect. Of course, there will always have to be an element of judgement and compromise. For maximum yield, one aims to sow seeds at the peak times of the relevant sidereal energy cycle, yet there is no point in doing so if the ground is too wet, too dry or too cold. Use the following information as a starting point to help you tap into the cosmic influences and improve your crops.

Identifying Your Crops

All plants can be divided into one of four groups, each related to one of the four elements: Earth, Water, Air and Fire.

EARTH
ROOT PLANTS

Asparagus	Horseradish	Onion	Spring onion
Beetroot (red beet)	Jerusalem artichoke	Parsnip	(scallion)
Carrot	Leek	Potato	Swede
Garlic	Mushroom	Radish	Turnip

WATER
LEAF PLANTS

Asparagus	Celery	Fennel	Rhubarb
Basil	Chicory (Belgian	Lettuce	Sage
Bay	endive)	Mint	Sorrel
Brussels sprout	Coriander	Mustard and cress	Spinach
Cabbage	Cress	Parsley	Thyme

AIR
FLOWERING PLANTS

Artichoke	Broccoli	Elderflower
Borage	Cauliflower	Flowering plants

FIRE
FRUIT-SEED PLANTS

Apple	Broad bean	French bean	Plum
Apricot	Cherry	Gooseberry	Pumpkin
Asparagus pea	Courgette	Marrow	Runner bean
Aubergine	(zucchini)	Nectarine	Sweetcorn (corn)
(eggplant)	Cucumber	Pea	Tomato
Blackberry	Fig	Pear	Vine

When to Sow, Cultivate and Harvest

For sowing crops, observe the four-element cycle. In the calendar, these are shown as Root, Leaf, Flower and Fruit-seed days. Use the lists above to identify the day on which your crop should be sown.

If convenient, sowings are best made on the day nearest to the middle of any of the three Moon signs of the appropriate element. Prepare the soil on the same day. Avoid sowing just before the Moon moves out of a sign. Such transition times are given to the nearest hour. In Australia, one of the fathers of bio-dynamics, Alex Podolinsky, advocates sowing just as the Moon enters a new Moon-sign element, so the seed has a full two days in that quality before it changes, on the grounds that it takes that long to germinate. That view may be important in drought-prone countries.

Bio-dynamic farmers believe that any disturbance of the soil should be carried out in the same Moon-sign element in which the seed was sown. Lettuce, for example, is sown on a Leaf day, so its soil preparation as well as subsequent thinning out, weeding and so on should also be done on a Leaf day to enhance the effect.

Both experiments and experience seem to suggest that harvesting as well as sowing should be done on the relevant element days, when the weather permits. For root crops to be stored over winter, harvest on a Root day nearest to the New Moon. Fortunately, there is no hurry in harvesting root crops, so you can usually select an optimum time.

Using the Star Rhythm

If, for practical reasons, you cannot sow at the optimum times, at least try to avoid the worst times. The following diagram shows the regular wave pattern followed by the cycle of the four elements.

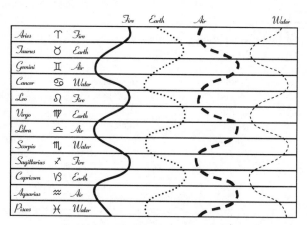

The four-element energy cycles

Root crops, for example, should ideally be sown during Earth days for optimal yield, but if this is impossible, try to avoid planting on days at the trough in the cycle when the Moon is in the opposite element, in this case Water days. The same principle applies to other elements.

The Best Times to Plant — Moonrise and Moonset

Gardeners are familiar with the idea that the time of day at which certain operations are performed is important. As the celestial element defines the best day for planting, Moonrise or Moonset suggests the best time of day to do the work. The calendar therefore indicates the time of Moonrise and Moonset each day, an hour either side being recommended as the best time to undertake any planting, working or gardening linked to the particular element of the day. Moonrise occurs in the daytime during the waxing phase, so this time is given for these dates. In the waning phase, Moonset occurs during the day, so this time is given. Thus Moonrise just before Full Moon happens in late afternoon. On the day of Full Moon, the Moon rises as the Sun sets.

Moonrise times are given for zero degrees longitude. For any other longitude, obtain the time of rising (GMT) by adding one hour per 15 degrees of longitude due west. If your position is three degrees due west, for example, add 12 minutes to the times given in the calendar. Also the Moon rises earlier due north. Readers in other latitudes can check this by watching the Moon rise and comparing the time of day to that given here.

Moonrise and Moonset are especially significant if a relevant aspect is being formed by the Moon that day, for example with the Sun or Saturn.

Laboratory research by US biologist Frank Brown has demonstrated that the greatest metabolic rate in both plants and small animals was registered at the times of Moonrise and culmination, when it reaches its highest point in the sky about six hours later. US traditions take these as the best times of day for fishing.

For effective lunar planting, seed should really begin to germinate as soon as it is sown by beginning to absorb moisture from the soil; so it is preferable, at least in warm weather, to sow seeds in the afternoon when the soil will remain moist for longer after sowing.

Planting out crops is, in general, best done in the evening so they have the night to settle in and rest, while pruning is best done in the morning so that the Sun will dry up the cut surface, thereby inhibiting bleeding. Traditionally, crops were harvested in the morning.

Grafting is generally a spring activity and pruning is one for late autumn and winter.

It is also recommended that pruning should be done on the waning Moon and grafting on the waxing Moon. Planting out should be done in the waxing Moon, if possible in the same element in which the sowings were made.

The Harmony of a Sun–Moon Trine

The calendar gives the trine (120°) angle between Sun and Moon, as happens twice a month. This is a harmonious aspect free of stress or conflict. Its moment of linking the two luminaries is a good time for many things. Like the event of Moonrise, it seems never before to have featured in a UK lunar-gardening guide: the idea came from the American book *Gardening Success with Lunar Aspects* by Adèle Barger (1976). This aspect is of particular interest for crops ruled by the Sun, for example oranges or vines.

Growing Flowers

For Flower days, the aspects between the Moon and Venus are given. A Moon–Venus energy is ideal for sowing or planting flowers, especially roses, which are ruled by Venus. The square aspects are also included, even though some might view them as unsuitable, expressing difficulty and stress. Alternatively, they could be viewed as assisting the development of structure, so it is up to you to choose.

Trees and Perennials

When working with trees or woody plants, choose a Saturn aspect for the most propitious time. The calendar gives three types of Moon–Saturn aspect each month: the opposition (180°), the trine (120°) and the sextile (60°). Growers should be mainly concerned with the Saturn aspects on Fruit-seed days, as most of their trees will be fruit-bearing. Because trees are going to last for years, there is all the more reason to identify the optimal date for planting. There may be a choice here: if planting a honeysuckle or clematis to grow up a wall, choose a Flower day, then look for either a Saturn aspect for durability or a Venus aspect for pretty flowers.

How to Read the Calendar

Each page is devoted to a single week, and each day provides all the essential information to help you make the most of your lunar gardening, indicated by various symbols. Each piece of information will be found in the same position on the daily calendars so they will soon become familiar. The calendar gives practical notes for the days to help your understanding of the aspects given, and makes suggestions on gardening activities. The notes also give the sacred Moons, such as when Easter falls or the Jewish New Year begins. Notice that the Muslim months begin a day or two after the actual New Moon, and these beginning days should be when you can first see the thin crescent of the New Moon at dusk. There's also space to record your own gardening notes.

The following symbols are used on the calendar. The key is repeated throughout the calendar along the bottom of the pages for easy reference.

Elements
These indicate the type of crop to sow on the relevant days.

 Earth – Root days   Air – Flower days

 Water – Leaf days   Fire – Fruit-seed days

Sidereal Signs
These show the zodiac sign relevant to the day, and the time at which the Moon moves into the next sign.

♈	Aries (Fire)	♎	Libra (Air)
♉	Taurus (Earth)	♏	Scorpio (Water)
♊	Gemini (Air)	♐	Sagittarius (Fire)
♋	Cancer (Water)	♑	Capricorn (Earth)
♌	Leo (Fire)	♒	Aquarius (Air)
♍	Virgo (Earth)	♓	Pisces (Water)

Moon Phases
Times are given next to the Moon symbols.

● New Moon   ○ Full Moon

◑ Waxing Moon, first quarter   ◐ Waning Moon, third quarter

Moonrise and Moonset
Although this information is not part of an ephemeris, times are given for Moonrise for the waxing Moon and Moonset for the waning Moon, as these occur during the day.

☾ Moonrise   ☽ Moonset

Aspects
Conjunction, opposition and square are considered negative aspects. Trine and sextile are considered positive aspects.

☌ Conjunction (0°)   □ Square (90°)

☍ Opposition (180°)   ✳ Sextile (60°)

△ Trine (120°)

Specific aspects are given that relate to Saturn, Venus and the Sun.

♄ Saturn   ☉ Sun

♀ Venus

Nodes
These are the points at which the Moon crosses the ecliptic.

☊   North node   ☋   South node

Apogee and Perigee
The apogee is the time at which the Moon is furthest from the Earth in its orbit, the perigee is when it is closest to the Earth.

$\mathcal{A}$ Apogee $\mathcal{P}$ Perigee

Understanding the Entries
Here are a couple of examples, showing how to read the daily entries.

Wednesday 24

Sow swedes or hardy turnips.

♑

○ 09.00

☾ 20.40

This is a Root day because the Moon is in Capricorn, an Earth constellation, shown by the zodiacal glyph on the left. The Moon-quarter symbol indicates that this is a Full Moon, its time to the nearest hour (GMT) noted next to the symbol. The time of Moonrise, to the nearest five minutes, is given next to the crescent.

Tuesday 27

♓ 12.00 ♈

☽ 09.40

☽ ⚹ ♄ 18.00

Change 12.00

The transition from one zodiac sign to another, the ingress, occurs at noon. As the Moon progresses through the zodiac, so the ruling elements shift according to the same timetable, so the morning is Pisces, a Water sign giving a Leaf day, while the afternoon is Aries, a Fire sign, giving a Fruit-seed day. Moonset is at 09.40, then in the afternoon there is a Moon-Saturn sextile (60°) aspect, which is good for trees.

Checklist for Using the Calendar

Annual crops
Follow the four-element rhythms, sowing as near to the centre of the relevant sign as is convenient. The same element-sign (Root, Leaf, Flower, Fruit-seed) reappears every nine days, so if you miss the appropriate period the next may still be convenient.

Grafting and transplanting

Try to do this kind of activity under a waxing Moon.

Harvesting

Fruits picked at New Moon will store better, whereas fruits to be eaten fresh are best picked at Full Moon. Crops should be harvested in the same Moon-sign element in which they were sown if you wish to obtain seeds for next year's crop.

Perennial crops, shrubs or trees

Try to take advantage of a Saturn–Moon aspect when planting. If a tree or bush is fruit-bearing, you can also try to plant or graft it on a Fruit-seed day.

Pruning and gelding

The lunar water uptake cycle is relevant here and near Full Moon is not recommended for pruning; try to time such activity for the waning Moon.

Sowing times

Sow and plant as close to the hour of Moonrise as possible, with adjustments to your longitude and latitude. Avoid sowing for a few hours either side of the nodes, the perigee or an eclipse. Where drought is a problem, note that seeds tend to absorb the greatest amount of water on the days prior to the Full Moon, so sowing at this time should lead to optimal germination.

Times and Time Zones

All times are given in the 24-hour clock. Aspect times are given to the nearest ten minutes, Moonrise and Moonset times to the nearest five minutes and other times to the nearest hour.

All times are GMT. For British Summer Time, add one hour to the given times. Users in other parts of the world will need to adjust the times according to their time zone, adding or subtracting the number of hours given below.

Time Zone Adjustments for North America		Time Zone Adjustments for Australasia	
Atlantic	-4 hours	New Zealand	+12 hours
Eastern	-5 hours	Western Australia	+ 8 hours
Central	-6 hours	Southern Australia	+ 9½ hours
Mountain	-7 hours	Northern Territory	+ 9½ hours
Pacific	-8 hours	New South Wales	+ 10 hours
Yukon	-9 hours	Victoria	+ 10 hours
Alaska-Hawaii	-10 hours	Queensland	+ 10 hours
Bering	-11 hours	Tasmania	+ 10 hours

October 2013

Tuesday 1	♋ 08.00 ♌ ☽ 15.50	Change 08.00
Wednesday 2	♌ ☽ 16.10 ☽ ✶ ♄ 14.10	
Thursday 3	♌ 17.00 ♍ ☽ 16.30 ☽ ✶ ♀ 18.50	Change 17.00
Friday 4 Dig up maincrop potatoes and beetroot for winter storage.	♍ ☽ 17.00	
Saturday 5 Harvest potatoes, onions and carrots for winter storage.	♍ 23.00 ♎ ● 01.00 ☾ 06.40	
Sunday 6 The Islamic month of *Zulhijah* begins.	♎ ☾ 07.50	

♄ Saturn	☉ Sun	☍ Opposition	✶ Sextile
♀ Venus	☌ Conjunction	☐ Square	△ Trine

October 2013

Monday 7

♎

☾ 09.00

☾ ☌ ♄ 03.00

Tuesday 8

Start planting winter lettuce around 10 am, and force-grow rhubarb in a warm greenhouse. Pick leafy herbs to store over winter.

♎ 03.00 ♏

☾ 10.20

☾ ☌ ♀ 14.00

Wednesday 9

Take cuttings of bay and rue. Divide roots of mint to re-plant elsewhere. Do grafting work with trees at 4–5 pm.

♏

☾ 11.20

☾ ✶ ☉ 16.30

Thursday 10

Pick late tomatoes and set aside to ripen on trays. Work on any fruit trees, especially around noon.

♏ 06.00 ♐

☾ 12.20

Friday 11

♐

PM only

◑

℗ 00.00

☾ 13.10

☾ ✶ ♄ 10.10

Saturday 12

♐ 09.00 ♑

☾ 13.50

Change 09.00

Sunday 13

A good day for preparing land and for digging compost into soil.

♑

☾ 14.30

☾ ✶ ♀ 04.00

● New Moon	◑ 1st quarter	☾ Moonrise	☊ North node	𝒜 Apogee
○ Full Moon	◐ 3rd quarter	☽ Moonset	☋ South node	℗ Perigee

October 2013

Monday 14

♑ 12.00 ♒

☾ 15.00

☾ △ ☉ 05.50

Change 12.00

Tuesday 15

A fine day for flowers and perennials: prepare new rose-beds or plant lily-of-the-valley in the evening. Lift and store summer flowering bulbs.

♒

☾ 15.20

☾ △ ♄ 16.50

Wednesday 16

♒ 16.00 ♓

☾ 15.50

Change 16.00

Thursday 17

The Sun meets the fortunate star Spica, as the sheaf of wheat held by the Virgin, linked traditionally to abundance and fertility.

♓

☾ 16.10

☾ △ ♀ 21.00

Friday 18

The Hunter's Moon, big and yellow, stays near to the horizon after rising; there is a partial lunar eclipse as it rises.

♓ 21.00 ♈

○ 23.00

☾ 16.40

Saturday 19

Harvest fruit to sell or to consume.

♈

☊ 23.00

☽ 07.00

AM only

Sunday 20

Prune fruit trees this afternoon. Pick and store apples and pears as they mature.

♈

☽ 08.10

☽ ☌ ♄ 06.00

♈	♉	♊	♋	♌	♍
Aries	Taurus	Gemini	Cancer	Leo	Virgo
Fire	*Earth*	*Air*	*Water*	*Fire*	*Earth*

October 2013

Monday 21
Cut out the fruited blackberry and loganberry canes and train in new shoots.

♈ 06.00 ♉

☽ 09.10

Tuesday 22

♉

☽ 10.10

Wednesday 23

♉ 17.00 ♊

☽ 11.00

☽ △ ☉ 05.30

Change 17.00

Thursday 24

♊

☽ 11.40

Friday 25
Prepare new rose beds. This morning is also good for indoor flower arranging.

♊

𝒜 14.00

☽ 12.20

☽ △ ♄ 05.10

Saturday 26
Pick winter lettuce in the afternoon.

♊ 05.00 ♋

◑

☽ 12.50

Sunday 27
BST ends.

♋

☽ 13.20

♎	♏	♐	♑	♒	♓
Libra	Scorpio	Sagittarius	Capricorn	Aquarius	Pisces
Air	Water	Fire	Earth	Air	Water

October 2013

Monday 28
Lunar eclipse.

♋ 17.00 ♌

☽ 13.50

☽ △ ♀ 12.20

Change 17.00

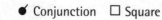

Tuesday 29
♌

☽ 14.10

☽ ✳ ☉ 16.10

Wednesday 30
♌

☽ 14.40

☽ ✳ ♄ 05.20

Thursday 31
Hallowe'en, traditionally a time of other-worldly interference in human affairs.

♌ 02.00 ♍

☽ 15.00

Gardening Notes

November Reminders ———

Friday 1

All Saints Day. Venus has climbed to its maximum elevation, so we see it as farthest from the Sun in the evening sky.

♍

☽ 15.30

Saturday 2

♍ 08.00 ♎

☽ 15.50

☽ ✶ ♀ 12.50

Change 08.00

Sunday 3

Total solar eclipse. *Diwali*, a five-day New Moon festival, begins. Wish your family and friends *Shubh Diwali* and light candles.

♎

● 13.00

☾ 06.40

☊ 06.00

No Planting

X

● New Moon	◑ 1st quarter	☾ Moonrise	☊ North node	⏀ Apogee
○ Full Moon	◐ 3rd quarter	☽ Moonset	☋ South node	⏀ Perigee

November 2013

Monday 4
Muharram, Islamic New Year – watch for the first sliver of the New Moon.

♎ 11.00 ♏

☽ 08.00

Change 11.00

Tuesday 5
Take the opportunity for a seasonal bonfire tonight.

♏

☽ 09.10

Wednesday 6

♏ 13.00 ♐

P 10.00

☽ 10.10

☽ ☌ ♄ 12.00

No Planting

✕

Thursday 7
Diwali ends. Today is the Cross-quarter pagan fire-festival of *Samhain*, a last gathering of the clans before winter sets in.

♐

☽ 11.10

Friday 8

♐ 14.00 ♑

☽ 11.50

Change 14.00

Saturday 9
Trim the growth of globe artichokes and draw soil around the crowns.

♑

☽ 12.30

Sunday 10

♑ 17.00 ♒

◑

☽ 13.00

Change 17.00

♈	♉	♊	♋	♌	♍
Aries	Taurus	Gemini	Cancer	Leo	Virgo
Fire	*Earth*	*Air*	*Water*	*Fire*	*Earth*

November 2013

Monday 11

Cut back and tidy any flowering plants around noon. In the greenhouse, start forcing bulbs and sow seed of most alpines. Finish planting roses.

♒

☾ 13.30

☾ ⚹ ♀ 12.50

Tuesday 12

♒ 22.00 ♓

☾ 13.50

☾ △ ♄ 04.40

Wednesday 13

♓

☾ 14.20

Thursday 14

♓

☾ 14.40

Friday 15

Plant gooseberry bushes and raspberry canes; sow round-seeded peas and prune trees.

♓ 05.00 ♈

☾ 15.10

Saturday 16

PM only

♈

☊ 03.00

☾ 15.40

☾ △ ♀ 10.00   ☾ ☌ ♄ 19.40

Sunday 17

♈ 14.00 ♉

○ 15.00

☾ 16.10

Change 14.00

♎	♏	♐	♑	♒	♓
Libra	Scorpio	Sagittarius	Capricorn	Aquarius	Pisces
Air	*Water*	*Fire*	*Earth*	*Air*	*Water*

November 2013

Monday 18
Finish digging new beds and borders for winter weathering.

♉

☽ 08.00

Tuesday 19
Turn over half-rotted compost and cover heavy land with rotted-down compost.

♉

☽ 08.50

Wednesday 20
Plant tulips, hardy climbers and roses, 9–10 am.

♉ 00.00 ♊

☽ 09.40

Thursday 21
Prick out any perennials you have raised in the greenhouse and sow winter bedding plants.

♊

☽ 10.20

☽ ☌ ♀ 16.50   ☽ △ ♄ 19.20

Friday 22

♊ 13.00 ♋

A 10.00

☽ 10.50

Change 13.00

Saturday 23
Take cuttings of bay and rue and place in pots of sand. Re-pot mint in the greenhouse.

♋

☽ 11.30

☽ ✳ ♄ 18.50

Sunday 24

♋

☽ 11.50

♄ Saturn   ☉ Sun   ☍ Opposition   ✳ Sextile

♀ Venus   ☌ Conjunction   □ Square   △ Trine

November/December 2013

Monday 25
Plant fruit trees and bushes. Soak dry tree roots before planting, and prune fruit trees after planting. Stake trees.

♋ 01.00 ♌
◑
☽ 12.10

Tuesday 26

♌
☽ 12.40
☽ ⚹ ♄ 20.40

Wednesday 27

♌ 12.00 ♍
☽ 13.00

Change 12.00

Thursday 28
Thanksgiving Day in the US.

♍
☽ 13.30
☽ ⚹ ☉ 09.40

Friday 29

♍ 18.00 ♎
☽ 13.50

Change 18.00

Saturday 30
St Andrew's Day.

♎
☊ 14.00
☽ 14.20

No Planting
X

Sunday 1
First Sunday in Advent. A fine flower-day with Saturn and Venus aspects. Prick out any perennials you have raised in the greenhouse.

♎ 21.00 ♏
☽ 15.00
☽ ☌ ♄ 09.10   ☽ ⚹ ♀ 17.10

| ● New Moon | ◑ 1st quarter | ☾ Moonrise | ☊ North node | 𝒜 Apogee |
| ○ Full Moon | ◐ 3rd quarter | ☽ Moonset | ☋ South node | 𝒫 Perigee |

December 2013

Monday 2
♏

☽ 15.50

Tuesday 3
♏ 22.00 ♐

● 00.00

☾ 08.00

Wednesday 4
The Islamic month of *Safar* begins today.

♐

℗ 10.00

☾ 09.00

No Planting

X

Thursday 5
AM: Sow melons for an early crop, and tomatoes for a summer crop in the greenhouse. Set any fruit trees.

♐ 22.00 ♑

☾ 09.50

☾ ⚹ ♄ 11.00

☾ ☌ ♀ 21.50

Friday 6
St Nicholas' Day, a time of surprise treats for children.

♑

☾ 10.30

Saturday 7
♑ 23.00 ♒

☾ 11.00

☾ ⚹ ☉ 08.00

Sunday 8
Sow winter bedding plants and pot autumn-sown sweet peas.

♒

☾ 11.30

♈	♉	♊	♋	♌	♍
Aries	Taurus	Gemini	Cancer	Leo	Virgo
Fire	*Earth*	*Air*	*Water*	*Fire*	*Earth*

December 2013

Monday 9

≋
◑
☾ 12.00
☾ △ ♄ 15.40

Tuesday 10

Venus is at her most brilliant in
the evening sky.

≋ 03.00 ♓
☾ 12.20
☾ ⚹ ♀ 06.40

Wednesday 11

Plant any hedges, shrubs and
trees around noon.

♓
☾ 12.50

Thursday 12

♓ 10.00 ♈
☾ 13.10

Change 10.00

Friday 13

Look eastwards after midnight
for Geminids meteor shower. Can
you see that it's multicoloured?

♈
☋ 07.00
☾ 13.40

PM only

Saturday 14

♈ 20.00 ♉
☾ 14.10
☾ ☌ ♄ 08.20

Change 20.00

Sunday 15

Check over any stored tubers for
signs of mould.

♉
☾ 14.50

♎	♏	♐	♑	≋	♓
Libra	Scorpio	Sagittarius	Capricorn	Aquarius	Pisces
Air	Water	Fire	Earth	Air	Water

December 2013

Monday 16	♉	
	☾ 15.40	

Tuesday 17 See how high the December Full Moon rises into the midnight sky.	♉ 07.00 ♊ ○ 09.00 ☾ 16.20	Change 07.00

Wednesday 18 Work with rose beds, pruning and finishing new planting. Plant shrubs if the weather permits.	♊ ☽ 08.20	

Thursday 19 Get ready for the winter solstice and put up mistletoe – a Druid 'solar' plant.	♊ 20.00 ♋ ☽ 08.50 ☽ △ ♄ 08.40	Change 20.00

Friday 20	♋ ☽ 09.30 ☽ ☌ ♀ 04.40	_A_ 00.00

Saturday 21 Midwinter solstice, at 5 pm, brings the longest night. The Sun crosses the Galactic Equator, of the Milky Way, at Zero–Capricorn.	♋ ☽ 10.00	

Sunday 22 Venus, still visible, goes retrograde, meaning it moves backwards against the stars.	♋ 08.00 ♌ ☽ 10.20	Change 08.00

♄ Saturn	☉ Sun	♂ Opposition	✳ Sextile
♀ Venus	☌ Conjunction	☐ Square	△ Trine

December 2013

Monday 23

Cut down old raspberry canes in the morning. Work on vines or other fruits in the greenhouse.

♌

☽ 10.40

Tuesday 24

♌ 20.00 ♍
◐
☽ 11.10
☽ ✶ ♄ 10.10

Change 20.00

Wednesday 25

This Christmas day the Moon is in the Virgin constellation, and there is a pleasant Moon–Venus trine for afternoon merriment.

♍

☽ 11.30

☽ △ ♀ 04.00

Thursday 26

Dispose of soft vegetable waste by digging it into trenches.

♍

☽ 11.50

Friday 27

♍ 04.00 ♎

☊ 22.00

☽ 12.20

AM only

Saturday 28

Trim back lawn edges to make the garden tidy.

♎

☽ 12.50

Sunday 29

♎ 08.00 ♏

☽ 13.30

☽ ✶ ♀ 13.50

Change 08.00

| ● New Moon | ◐ 1st quarter | ☾ Moonrise | ☊ North node | A Apogee |
| ○ Full Moon | ◐ 3rd quarter | ☽ Moonset | ☋ South node | P Perigee |

December 2013

Monday 30

♏

☾ 02.20

Tuesday 31

New Year's Eve – can you see the
old, dying moon set at 3 pm?

♏ 09.00 ♐

☾ 03.30

Change 09.00

Gardening Notes ————

♈	♉	♊	♋	♌	♍
Aries	Taurus	Gemini	Cancer	Leo	Virgo
Fire	*Earth*	*Air*	*Water*	*Fire*	*Earth*

January 2014

January Reminders

Wednesday 1 New Year's Day	♐ ● 11.00 ☾ 07.30	P 22.00	AM only
Thursday 2 Watch out for meteor showers.	♐ 08.00 ♑ ☾ 08.20 ☾ ● ♀ 11.10		Change 08.00
Friday 3 The Islamic month of *R'Athwal* begins. See the thin crescent of the New Moon.	♑ ☾ 09.00 ☾ ● ♀ 11.10		
Saturday 4 Earth reaches Perihelion at 12 noon – our annual nearest approach to the Sun.	♑ 08.00 ♒ ☾ 09.30		Change 08.00
Sunday 5 On Twelfth Night Jupiter shines brightest, while Venus vanishes as the Evening Star.	♒ ☾ 10.00		

♎	♏	♐	♑	♒	♓
Libra *Air*	Scorpio *Water*	Sagittarius *Fire*	Capricorn *Earth*	Aquarius *Air*	Pisces *Water*

January 2014

Monday 6

Epiphany, when gifts of Gold, Frankincense and Myrrh were brought by the three Magi ('astrologers') to the baby Jesus.

≈ 10.00 ♓

☽ 10.30

☽ ⚹ ♀ 09.50

Change 10.00

Tuesday 7

♓

☽ 10.50

Wednesday 8

♓ 16.00 ♈

◑

☽ 11.20

Change 16.00

Thursday 9

♈

☊ 10.00

☽ 11.50

No Planting

Friday 10

A Fruit day with a trine to Venus: work in the greenhouse with fruit/seed crops.

♈

☽ 12.20

☽ ☍ ♄ 19.00

☽ △ ♀ 20.00

Saturday 11

♈ 02.00 ♉

☽ 12.50

☽ ⚹ ♄ 10.40

Sunday 12

♉

☽ 13.30

| ♄ Saturn | ☉ Sun | ☍ Opposition | ⚹ Sextile |
| ♀ Venus | ☌ Conjunction | ☐ Square | △ Trine |

January 2014

Monday 13
Chit seed potatoes in the greenhouse this morning.

♉ 13.00 ♊

☽ 14.20

Change 13.00

Tuesday 14

♊

☽ 15.10

Wednesday 15

♊

☽ 16.10

☽ ☌ ♀ 14.10

Thursday 16
At midnight notice how high the full moon rises. Later, see Venus as the Morning Star.

♊ 02.00 ♋

○ 05.00

𝒜 02.00

☽ 17.10

Friday 17

♋

☽ 08.00

Saturday 18

♋ 14.00 ♌

☽ 08.30

Change 14.00

Sunday 19

♌

☽ 08.50

● New Moon ◐ 1st quarter ☾ Moonrise ☊ North node 𝒜 Apogee
○ Full Moon ◑ 3rd quarter ☽ Moonset ☋ South node 𝒫 Perigee

January 2014

Monday 20 ♌

☽ 09.10

☽ △ ♀ 09.40

Tuesday 21 ♌ 02.00 ♍

☽ 09.40

Wednesday 22 ♍

Dig over the soil today.

☽ 10.00

Thursday 23 ♍ 11.00 ♎

◐

☽ 10.20

Change 11.00

Friday 24 ♎

PM only

☊ 03.00

☽ 10.50

Saturday 25 ♎ 18.00 ♏

Burns' Night. *My love is like a red, red rose...* Mark the day with some haggis.

Change 18.00

☽ 11.30

☽ ☌ ♄ 13.40

Sunday 26 ♏

Time to sow early salad crops in the greenhouse, at the moonrise hour of noon if possible.

☽ 12.10

☽ ⚹ ☉ 14.20

♈	♉	♊	♋	♌	♍
Aries	Taurus	Gemini	Cancer	Leo	Virgo
Fire	*Earth*	*Air*	*Water*	*Fire*	*Earth*

January 2014

Monday 27

♏ 20.00 ♐

☽ 13.00

Tuesday 28

Sow fruit crops in the greenhouse, using the moonrise hour of 2 pm.

♐

☽ 14.10

☽ ☌ ♀ 22.00

Wednesday 29

♐ 20.00 ♑

☽ 15.40

☽ ⚹ ♄ 16.40

Change 20.00

Thursday 30

The Moon is at perigee so keep out of garden.

♑

● 22.00   ℗ 10.00

☾ 06.50

No Planting

Friday 31

Chinese New Year – the year of the Horse. Make a fresh start by clearing out clutter and paying off debts.

♑ 19.00 ♒

☾ 07.30

Change 19.00

Gardening Notes

♎	♏	♐	♑	♒	♓
Libra	Scorpio	Sagittarius	Capricorn	Aquarius	Pisces
Air	*Water*	*Fire*	*Earth*	*Air*	*Water*

February 2014

Saturday 1

The Islamic month of *R'Akhir* begins today.

≈

☾ 08.00

Sunday 2

Candlemas, or Groundhog Day in America when groundhogs emerge from hibernation.

≈ 20.00 ♓

☾ 08.30

Change 20.00

| ♄ Saturn | ⊙ Sun | ☍ Opposition | ⚹ Sextile |
| ♀ Venus | ☌ Conjunction | ☐ Square | △ Trine |

February 2014

Monday 3

The old English fire-festival of Imbolc marks winter's end and signifies the first glimpse of spring. Mark the occasion with a log-fire.

♓

☾ 08.50

Tuesday 4

♓ 24.00 ♈

☾ 09.20

☾ ⚹ ☉ 07.30

Wednesday 5

♈

☋ 14.00

☾ 09.50

No Planting

✗

Thursday 6

Sow early peas and broad beans under cloches in a sheltered area, 10am–noon.

♈

☾ 10.20

☾ △ ♀ 12.10

Friday 7

♈ 08.00 ♉

☾ 10.50

Change 08.00

Saturday 8

♉

☾ 11.30

Sunday 9

♉ 19.00 ♊

☾ 12.20

☾ △ ☉ 11.40

Change 19.00

● New Moon	◑ 1st quarter	☾ Moonrise	☊ North node	𝒜 Apogee
○ Full Moon	◐ 3rd quarter	☽ Moonset	☋ South node	𝒫 Perigee

February 2014

Monday 10
Sow early seeds for spring flowers.

♊

☾ 13.10

Tuesday 11
Venus reaches her greatest brilliance as the Morning Star.

♊

☾ 14.00

☾ ☋ ♀ 13.00

Wednesday 12

♊ 08.00 ♋

𝒜 06.00

☾ 15.00

Change 08.00

Thursday 13
Clear dead material from leafy plants; sow salad crops under glass or in plastic cloches.

♋

☾ 16.00

Friday 14

♋ 20.00 ♌

○ 24.00

☾ 17.10

Saturday 15
Buddhist Nirvana Day.

♌

☽ 07.00

Sunday 16

♌

☽ 07.20

♈	♉	♊	♋	♌	♍
Aries	Taurus	Gemini	Cancer	Leo	Virgo
Fire	*Earth*	*Air*	*Water*	*Fire*	*Earth*

February 2014

Monday 17

♌ 08.00 ♍

☽ 07.40

☽ ⚹ ♄ 05.00

Change 08.00

Tuesday 18

Sow parsnips, garlic, carrots or radishes.

♍

☽ 08.00

Wednesday 19

♍ 17.00 ♎

☽ 08.30

Change 17.00

Thursday 20

Avoid the garden this morning under the north node.

♎

☊ 07.00

☽ 09.00

PM only

Friday 21

♎

☽ 09.30

☽ ⚹ ♀ 18.00

Saturday 22

Sow seeds for foliage plants in the greenhouse.

♎ 00.00 ♏

◑

☽ 10.10

Sunday 23

♏

☽ 11.00

♎	♏	♐	♑	♒	♓
Libra	Scorpio	Sagittarius	Capricorn	Aquarius	Pisces
Air	*Water*	*Fire*	*Earth*	*Air*	*Water*

February 2014

Monday 24	♏ 05.00 ♐ ☽ 11.50	

Tuesday 25	♐ ☽ 13.00	

Wednesday 26	♐ 06.00 ♑ ☽ 14.10	Change 06.00

Thursday 27 It's perigee this afternoon so keep out of garden.	♑ ♇ 20.00 ☽ 15.40	AM only

Friday 28 New Moon is a time to prune or cut back trees.	♑ 06.00 ♒ ☽ 17.00	Change 06.00

Gardening Notes

♄ Saturn	☉ Sun	☍ Opposition	✳ Sextile
♀ Venus	☌ Conjunction	☐ Square	△ Trine

March 2014

March Reminders

Saturday 1	≋	
St David's Day	● 08.00	
	☾ 06.20	

Sunday 2	≋ 07.00 ♓	
	☾ 06.50	Change 07.00
	☾ ✳ ♀ 11.00	

● New Moon	◑ 1st quarter	☾ Moonrise	☊ North node	*A* Apogee
○ Full Moon	◑ 3rd quarter	☽ Moonset	☋ South node	*P* Perigee

March 2014

Monday 3
The Islamic month of *J'Awal* starts today.

♓

☾ 07.20

Tuesday 4
Shrove Tuesday – or Mardi Gras 'fat Tuesday'.

♓ 10.00 ♈

☊ 21.00

☾ 07.50

AM only

Wednesday 5
Ash Wednesday, the first day of Lent. Consider giving up eggs, milk or cheese to help the creatures that are breeding.

♈

☾ 08.20

Thursday 6

♈ 16.00 ♉

☾ 08.50

Change 16.00

Friday 7

♉

☾ 09.30

Saturday 8

♉

☾ 10.10

Sunday 9

♉ 03.00 ♊

◑

☾ 11.00

♈	♉	♊	♋	♌	♍
Aries	Taurus	Gemini	Cancer	Leo	Virgo
Fire	Earth	Air	Water	Fire	Earth

March 2014

Monday 10
Sow flowers around noon.

♊

☾ 12.00

Tuesday 11

♊ 15.00 ♋

♪ 20.00

☾ 12.50

Change 15.00

Wednesday 12
Sow salad crops under glass or in plastic cloches, around 2 pm.

♋

☾ 13.50

☾ ☊ ♀ 14.00

Thursday 13

♋

☾ 15.00

Friday 14
See how things start to grow and germinate coming up to the Full Moon, especially if there has been some rain.

♋ 03.00 ♌

☾ 16.00

Saturday 15

♌

☾ 17.00

Sunday 16
The mating of farm animals will be more successful around the spring Full Moons.

♌ 14.00 ♍

○ 07.00

☾ 18.10

☾ ✳ ♄ 11.30

Change 14.00

♎	♏	♐	♑	♒	♓
Libra	Scorpio	Sagittarius	Capricorn	Aquarius	Pisces
Air	Water	Fire	Earth	Air	Water

March 2014

Monday 17
St Patrick's Day. Perhaps enjoy a Guinness?

♍

☽ 06.10

☽ △ ♀ 21.10

Tuesday 18

♍ 23.00 ♎

☽ 06.40

Wednesday 19

♎

♌ 10.00

☽ 07.00

No Planting

✗

Thursday 20
Spring Equinox at 5 pm, when the day and night are of equal length.

♎

☽ 07.30

Friday 21
Persian New Year.

♎ 06.00 ♏

☽ 08.10

Saturday 22
Venus rises highest in the sky.

♏

☽ 09.00

☽ ✶ ♀ 19.00

Sunday 23

♏ 11.00 ♐

◖

☽ 09.40

Change 11.00

♄ Saturn   ☉ Sun   ⚊ Opposition   ✶ Sextile

♀ Venus   ● Conjunction   ☐ Square   △ Trine

March 2014

Monday 24	♐	
	☽ 10.50	
Tuesday 25	♐ 13.00 ♑	
	☽ 12.00	Change 13.00
	☽ ✶ ♄ 10.50	
Wednesday 26 Good Root day with Sun and Moon chiming in the morning.	♑	
	☽ 13.10	
	☽ ✶ ☉ 08.00	
Thursday 27	♑ 15.00 ♒	AM only
	℘ 18.00	
	☽ 14.30	
	☽ ☌ ♀ 07.50	
Friday 28 See the dying old Moon set at 5–6 pm.	♒	
	☽ 15.50	
Saturday 29	♒ 17.00 ♓	
	☽ 17.10	Change 17.00
Sunday 30 Mothering Sunday – spend time with Mum, or perhaps visit the church where you were baptised. British Summer Time begins.	♓	
	● 19.00	
	☾ 05.20	

● New Moon	◗ 1st quarter	☾ Moonrise	☊ North node	⍺ Apogee
○ Full Moon	◐ 3rd quarter	☽ Moonset	☋ South node	℘ Perigee

March/April 2014

Monday 31
Hindu New Year.

♓ 19.00 ♈

☾ 05.50
☾ ⚹ ♀ 20.00

Change 19.00

Tuesday 1
The Islamic month of *J'Akir* begins.

♈

☊ 04.00

☾ 05.10

PM only

Wednesday 2

♈

☾ 05.50

Thursday 3

♈ 01.00 ♉

☾ 06.20

Friday 4

♉

☾ 07.10
☾ ⚹ ☉ 16.00

Saturday 5
Plant onion sets and sow parsnips in the early morning.

♉ 10.00 ♊

☾ 07.50
☾ △ ♀ 21.40

Change 10.00

Sunday 6

♊

☾ 08.50

♈	♉	♊	♋	♌	♍
Aries	Taurus	Gemini	Cancer	Leo	Virgo
Fire	*Earth*	*Air*	*Water*	*Fire*	*Earth*

April 2014

Monday 7

♊ 22.00 ♋
◐
☾ 09.40

Tuesday 8

Mars glows brightest in the sky.

♋

♈ 15.00

☾ 10.40

Wednesday 9

♋

☾ 11.40

Thursday 10

♋ 10.00 ♌

☾ 12.50

Change 10.00

Friday 11

Sow tomatoes on a warm windowsill today.

♌

☾ 13.50

☾ ☊ ♀ 09.50

Saturday 12

♌ 21.00 ♍

☾ 15.00

☾ ✶ ♄ 17.10

Sunday 13

Palm Sunday, Holy Week begins. Graft during the waxing moon, preferably around the moonrise hour.

♍

☾ 16.00

April 2014

Monday 14

♍

☾ 17.10

Tuesday 15

Total lunar eclipse at the Easter Full moon: stay out of the garden.

♍ 05.00 ♎

○ 06.00   ☋ 13.00

☾ 18.20

No Planting

✗

Wednesday 16

A fine Flower day with Moon trine to Venus around noon.

♎

☽ 06.30

☽ △ ♀ 13.00

Thursday 17

♎ 11.00 ♏

☽ 07.10

☽ ☌ ♄ 07.10

Change 11.00

Friday 18

Good Friday.

♏

☽ 07.50

Saturday 19

♏ 15.00 ♐

☽ 08.40

Change 15.00

Sunday 20

Easter Sunday, the spring day of Resurrection.

♐

☽ 09.40

| ♄ Saturn | ☉ Sun | ♂ Opposition | ✳ Sextile |
| ♀ Venus | ● Conjunction | □ Square | △ Trine |

April 2014

Monday 21
Bank Holiday.

♐ 18.00 ♑

◐

☽ 10.50

☽ ✶ ♄ 13.50

Change 18.00

Tuesday 22
The world honours Earth-Day today.

♑

℘ 23.00

☽ 12.00

AM only

Wednesday 23
St George's Day,

♑ 21.00 ♒

☽ 13.10

Thursday 24

♒

☽ 14.30

☽ ✶ ☉ 14.10

Friday 25
Tend to flowering perennials this afternoon. Prune out dead wood during this waning Moon.

♒ 24.00 ♓

☽ 15.50

Saturday 26
Sow lettuce around 5 pm.

♓

☽ 17.10

Sunday 27

♓

☽ 18.20

● New Moon ◐ 1st quarter ☾ Moonrise ☊ North node 𝒜 Apogee
○ Full Moon ◑ 3rd quarter ☽ Moonset ☋ South node ℘ Perigee

April 2014

Monday 28

♓ 04.00 ♈

♋ 10.00

☽ 19.30

No Planting

✗

Tuesday 29
Annular solar eclipse.

♈

● 06.00

☾ 03.40

Wednesday 30
The Islamic month of *Rajab* begins.

♈ 10.00 ♉

☾ 04.20

☾ ⚹ ♀ 15.50

Change 10.00

Gardening Notes

♈	♉	♊	♋	♌	♍
Aries	Taurus	Gemini	Cancer	Leo	Virgo
Fire	*Earth*	*Air*	*Water*	*Fire*	*Earth*

May 2014

May Reminders ——————————

Thursday 1

On May Day, a May Queen
honours the fertility of the Earth.
Party all night, if you can.

☿   radishes in Tire

☾ 06.00

Friday 2

♉ 20.00 ♊

☾ 06.40

Change 20.00

Saturday 3

♊

☾ 07.40

Sunday 4

♊

☾ 08.30

☾ ✶ ☉ 09.30

♎	♏	♐	♑	♒	♓
Libra	Scorpio	Sagittarius	Capricorn	Aquarius	Pisces
Air	Water	Fire	Earth	Air	Water

May 2014

Monday 5

The quarter-day pagan fire-festival of Beltane, when young people jump over the flames and elders drink mead (Bank holiday).

♊ 07.00 ♋

☾ 09.30

Change 07.00

Tuesday 6

♋

♃ 10.00

☾ 10.30

Wednesday 7

♋ 19.00 ♌

◑

☾ 11.30

Change 19.00

Thursday 8

Sow runner beans and set up canes to support them. See the old Moon dying in the twilight.

♌

☾ 12.30

Friday 9

♌

☾ 13.40   ·

Saturday 10

Cold Saturn is brightest in the sky around now.

♌ 07.00 ♍

☾ 14.40

☉ ☌ ♄ 18.30

Change 07.00

Sunday 11

♍

☾ 15.50

| ♄ Saturn | ☉ Sun | ♂ Opposition | ✶ Sextile |
| ♀ Venus | ☌ Conjunction | □ Square | △ Trine |

May 2014

Monday 12

♍ 15.00 ♎

☊ 20.00

AM only

☾ 17.00

☾ ☌ ♀ 11.30

Tuesday 13

Sow hardy and half-hardy annuals when all possible risk of frost has passed.

♎

☾ 18.10

Wednesday 14

The mating of animals may be particularly successful around this Full-Moon period. Wesak, the Buddha's Birthday.

♎ 20.00 ♏

○ 19.00

☾ 19.20

☾ ☌ ♄ 12.00

Thursday 15

Sow lettuce thinly where it can benefit from afternoon shade from taller plants.

♏

☽ 05.50

Friday 16

The Sun meets the binary star Algol 'Medusa's head', so tell a horror-story today.

♏ 23.00 ♐

☽ 06.40

☽ △ ♀ 07.20

Saturday 17

♐

☽ 07.30

Sunday 18

♐

No Planting

𝒫 12.00

☽ 08.40

☽ ✳ ♄ 16.20

X

● New Moon	◐ 1st quarter	☾ Moonrise	☊ North node	𝒜 Apogee
○ Full Moon	◑ 3rd quarter	☽ Moonset	☋ South node	𝒫 Perigee

May 2014

Monday 19

♐ 01.00 ♑

☽ 09.50

☽ △ ☉ 07.00

Tuesday 20

♑

☽ 11.10

☽ ⚹ ♀ 20.00

Wednesday 21

♑ 03.00 ♒

◑

☽ 12.20

Thursday 22

Prune lilac bushes especially if
they have finished flowering.

♒

☽ 13.40

Friday 23

♒ 06.00 ♓

☽ 14.50

Change 06.00

Saturday 24

♓

☽ 16.10

Sunday 25

Keep out of the garden today
under the south node.

♓ 12.00 ♈

☋ 16.00

☽ 17.20

No Planting

X

♈	♉	♊	♋	♌	♍
Aries	Taurus	Gemini	Cancer	Leo	Virgo
Fire	*Earth*	*Air*	*Water*	*Fire*	*Earth*

May 2014

Monday 26
Spring Bank holiday. Watch the last sliver of the old moon disappear before sunset.

♈

☽ 18.30

Tuesday 27

♈ 19.00 ♉

☽ 19.40

Change 19.00

Wednesday 28

♉

● 19.00

☾ 03.50

Thursday 29
The Islamic month of *Syaaban* starts today.

♉

☾ 04.40

☾ ⚹ ♀ 18.00

Friday 30
The Sun meets Aldebaran the rose-pink 'Bull's Eye' bringing good fortune. Plant out cauliflowers, especially if the soil is moist.

♉ 04.00 ♊

☾ 05.30

Saturday 31

♊

☾ 06.20

♎	♏	♐	♑	♒	♓
Libra	Scorpio	Sagittarius	Capricorn	Aquarius	Pisces
Air	*Water*	*Fire*	*Earth*	*Air*	*Water*

Sunday 1

♊ 15.00 ♋

☾ 07.20

Change 15.00

♄ Saturn	☉ Sun	☍ Opposition	✳ Sextile
♀ Venus	☌ Conjunction	☐ Square	△ Trine

June 2014

Monday 2
♋
☾ 08.20

Tuesday 3
♋
𝒜 04.00
☾ 09.20

Wednesday 4
Continue to sow dwarf and runner beans.

♋ 03.00 ♌
☾ 10.20

Thursday 5
A fine day for Fruit-seed crops with a trine to Venus in the morning.

♌
◑
☾ 11.20
☾ △ ♀ 07.20

Friday 6
♌ 15.00 ♍
☾ 12.30

Change 15.00

Saturday 7
The Moon is close to Mars in the sky after sunset.

♍
☾ 13.30

Sunday 8
Today has the harmony of a Sun-Moon trine at noon.

♍
☾ 14.40
☾ △ ☉ 11.40

● New Moon   ◐ 1st quarter   ☾ Moonrise   ☊ North node   𝒜 Apogee
○ Full Moon   ◑ 3rd quarter   ☽ Moonset   ☋ South node   𝒫 Perigee

June 2014

Monday 9

♍ 01.00 ♎

♌ 03.00

☾ 15.50

PM only

Tuesday 10

♎

☾ 17.00

☾ ☋ ♀ 12.50   ☾ ☌ ♄ 16.30

Wednesday 11

♎ 06.00 ♏

Pinch out shoots on aromatics such as rosemary to encourage growth.

☾ 18.10

Thursday 12

♏

☾ 19.20

Friday 13

♏ 08.00 ♐

The Full Moon is a fine time for the mating of animals. See how low it stays in the night sky, compared to the winter moons.

○ 04.00

☾ 20.20

Change 08.00

Saturday 14

♐

☽ 06.20

Sunday 15

♐ 09.00 ♑

℘ 04.00

☽ 07.50

PM only

♈	♉	♊	♋	♌	♍
Aries	Taurus	Gemini	Cancer	Leo	Virgo
Fire	*Earth*	*Air*	*Water*	*Fire*	*Earth*

June 2014

Monday 16
Take softwood cuttings of shrubs to make new plants.

♑

☽ 08.50

Tuesday 17

♑ 09.00 ♒

☽ 10.10

☽ △ ☉ 12.10

Change 09.00

Wednesday 18
Sow hardy wild flowers, hoe for weeds and sow wallflowers, using the moonset hour of 11.30 am.

♒

☽ 11.30

Thursday 19

♒ 12.00 ♓

◑

☽ 12.50

☽ ✳ ♀ 13.10

Change 12.00

Friday 20

♓

☽ 14.00

Saturday 21
Celebrate the summer solstice at 11 am with some friends, it's the longest day.

♓ 17.00 ♈

☋ 18.00

☽ 15.10

AM only

Sunday 22

♈

☽ 16.10

☽ ✳ ☉ 04.10

♎	♏	♐	♑	♒	♓
Libra	Scorpio	Sagittarius	Capricorn	Aquarius	Pisces
Air	*Water*	*Fire*	*Earth*	*Air*	*Water*

June 2014

Monday 23

Tend to fruit trees in the morning, under the Saturn-opposition.

♈

☽ 17.30

Tuesday 24

St John's day – like Christmas, this happens a few days after the solstice.

♈ 01.00 ♉

☽ 18.30

☽ ☌ ♀ 13.30

Wednesday 25

♉

☽ 19.30

Thursday 26

♉ 10.00 ♊

☽ 20.20

Change 10.00

Friday 27

Plant Brussels sprouts, winter cabbage, savoys and both purple-sprouting and spring-headed broccoli.

♊

● 08.00

☾ 04.10

Saturday 28

Ramadan begins, when Muslims fast from dawn till dusk.

♊ 22.00 ♋

☾ 05.10

Sunday 29

♋

☾ 06.10

♄ Saturn   ☉ Sun   ☍ Opposition   ✳ Sextile

♀ Venus   ☌ Conjunction   ☐ Square   △ Trine

June/July 2014

Monday 30
Harvest salad and soft herbs to encourage new growth.

♋

☾ 07.10

Tuesday 1

♋ 10.00 ♌

☾ 08.10

Change 10.00

Wednesday 2

♌

☾ 09.10

☾ ✶ ☉ 17.10

Thursday 3
Aphelion, an annual event when the Earth has moved furthest away from the Sun.

♌ 23.00 ♍

☾ 10.10

Friday 4

♍

◐

☾ 11.20

Saturday 5

♍

☾ 12.20

☾ △ ♀ 13.50

Sunday 6

♍ 09.00 ♎

☋ 09.00

☾ 13.30

No Planting

✗

● New Moon   ◐ 1st quarter   ☾ Moonrise   ☊ North node   𝒜 Apogee
○ Full Moon   ◑ 3rd quarter   ☽ Moonset   ☋ South node   𝒫 Perigee

July 2014

Monday 7
Use the moonrise hour of 2–3 pm to plant flowers.

♎

☾ 14.40

Tuesday 8
♎ 16.00 ♏

☾ 15.50

Change 16.00

Wednesday 9
♏

☾ 17.00

Thursday 10
See the last sliver of the old Moon at sunset.

♏ 18.00 ♐

☾ 18.00

☾ ● ♀ 11.20

Change 18.00

Friday 11
♐

☾ 19.00

Saturday 12
Full moon at perigee, close to aphelion – this alignment could produce floods.

♐ 18.00 ♑

○ 11.00

☾ 19.50

Change 18.00

Sunday 13
♑

ℙ 08.00

☾ 06.30

PM only

♈	♉	♊	♋	♌	♍
Aries	Taurus	Gemini	Cancer	Leo	Virgo
Fire	*Earth*	*Air*	*Water*	*Fire*	*Earth*

July 2014

Monday 14

♑ 18.00 ♒

☽ 07.50

☽ △ ♀ 19.20

Change 18.00

Tuesday 15

A good flower day so tend annuals and perennials.

♒

☽ 09.10

Wednesday 16

♒ 19.00 ♓

☽ 10.30

☽ △ ☉ 18.10

Change 19.00

Thursday 17

♓

☽ 11.50

Friday 18

♓ 23.00 ♈

☊ 22.00

☽ 13.00

AM only

Saturday 19

♈

◐

☽ 14.10

☽ ✶ ♀ 10.30

Sunday 20

Prune apple and pear trees today, and thin early dessert apples.

♈

☽ 15.20

♎	♏	♐	♑	♒	♓
Libra	Scorpio	Sagittarius	Capricorn	Aquarius	Pisces
Air	*Water*	*Fire*	*Earth*	*Air*	*Water*

July 2014

Monday 21

♈ 06.00 ♉

☽ 16.20
☽ ✳ ☉ 14.10

Change 06.00

Tuesday 22

Use the moonset hour for earthing-up maincrop potatoes and Jerusalem artichokes, and sow turnips for winter use.

♉

☽ 17.20

Wednesday 23

♉ 16.00 ♊

☽ 18.10

Change 16.00

Thursday 24

Lift and divide hellebores in a moist, shady spot. Use the Venus-conjunction this afternoon.

♊

☽ 19.00
☽ ☌ ♀ 17.42

Friday 25

Tend to perennial flowers and bushes, sowing or transplanting them around noon.

♊

☽ 19.40

Saturday 26

♊ 04.00 ♋
● 23.00
☾ 04.00

Sunday 27

Sow lettuce and greens for winter use: leeks, late Brussels sprouts, winter cabbage, sprouting and spring broccoli.

♋

☾ 05.00

♄ Saturn   ☉ Sun   ☍ Opposition   ✳ Sextile

♀ Venus   ☌ Conjunction   □ Square   △ Trine

July 2014

Monday 28

Eid al-Fitr, the end of Ramadan, then the Islamic month of *Syawal* begins. Watch for a meteor shower tonight.

♋ 16.00 ♌

𝒜 04.00

☾ 06.00

Change 16.00

Tuesday 29

♌

☾ 07.00

Wednesday 30

♌

☾ 08.00

☾ ✶ ♀ 08.30   ☾ ✶ ♄ 13.30

Thursday 31

♌ 05.00 ♍

☾ 09.10

Gardening Notes

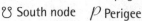

August 2014

August Reminders

Friday 1

♍

☾ 10.10

☾ ⚹ ☉ 10.10

Saturday 2

Avoid gardening today. Perhaps enjoy a meal al-fresco if the weather is good?

♍ 16.00 ♎

♌ 13.00

☾ 11.20

No Planting

✗

Sunday 3

♎

◑

☾ 12.20

♈	♉	♊	♋	♌	♍
Aries	Taurus	Gemini	Cancer	Leo	Virgo
Fire	*Earth*	*Air*	*Water*	*Fire*	*Earth*

August 2014

Monday 4

♎︎

☽ 13.30

☽ ☌ ♄ 10.20   ☽ △ ♀ 17.40

Tuesday 5

Transplant flower seedlings this afternoon, plant daffodils and take cuttings from rambling roses.

♎︎ 24.00 ♏︎

☽ 14.40

Wednesday 6

♏︎

☽ 15.40

☽ △ ☉ 10.30

Thursday 7

Today is Lammas, the old English harvest-time festival and the essential holiday season. Enjoy a barbecue.

♏︎ 04.00 ♐︎

☽ 16.40

Friday 8

Re-pot tomatoes sown in June. Prepare the ground for planting new fruit stocks, and complete the planting of strawberry runners.

♐︎

☽ 17.30

☽ ✶ ♄ 17.00

Saturday 9

♐︎ 05.00 ♑︎

☽ 18.20

☽ ☍ ♀ 08.00

Sunday 10

Proxigee (closest Perigee of the year) at Full Moon brings strong pull of gravity – danger of floods.

♑︎

○ 18.00   ℗ 18.00

☽ 19.00

AM only

♎︎	♏︎	♐︎	♑︎	♒︎	♓︎
Libra	Scorpio	Sagittarius	Capricorn	Aquarius	Pisces
Air	*Water*	*Fire*	*Earth*	*Air*	*Water*

August 2014

Monday 11

A day for sowing wallflowers and Sweet Williams for next year. Prune rambling roses.

♑ 04.00 ♒

☽ 06.40

Tuesday 12

Stay up till midnight to see the sparky Perseids meteor shower.

♒

☽ 08.00

Wednesday 13

♒ 04.00 ♓

☽ 09.20

☽ △ ♀ 15.40

Thursday 14

♓

☽ 10.40

Friday 15

♓ 06.00 ♈

☊ 03.00

☽ 12.00

PM only

Saturday 16

Prune the fruited shoots of peach and plum trees.

♈

☽ 13.10

Sunday 17

♈ 12.00 ♉

☽ 14.10

Change 12.00

♄ Saturn	☉ Sun	♂ Opposition	⚹ Sextile
♀ Venus	☌ Conjunction	☐ Square	△ Trine

August 2014

Monday 18
See the Venus–Saturn conjunction in the early-morning sky.

♉

☽ 15.20

☽ ⚹ ♀ 13.10

Tuesday 19
♉ 22.00 ♊

☽ 16.10

Wednesday 20
♊

☽ 16.50

Thursday 21
Tend to roses and perennial flowers and bushes in the afternoon.

♊

☽ 17.40

Friday 22
♊ 10.00 ♋

☽ 18.10

Change 10.00

Saturday 23
♋

☽ 18.50

Sunday 24
Sow lettuce and spring cabbage if the soil is not too dry.

♋ 22.00 ♌

𝒜 06.00

☽ 19.00

● New Moon ◐ 1st quarter ☾ Moonrise ☊ North node 𝒜 Apogee

○ Full Moon ◑ 3rd quarter ☽ Moonset ☋ South node 𝒫 Perigee

August 2014

Monday 25
Bank holiday.

♌

● 14.00

☾ 04.50

Tuesday 26
Crops harvested at New Moon will keep best. Dry out herbs before storing them.

♌

☾ 06.00

Wednesday 27
The Islamic month of *Zukeadah* begins today.

♌ 11.00 ♍

☾ 07.00

Change 11.00

Thursday 28

♍

☾ 08.00

Friday 29
Prune evergreen hedges by the end of the month.

♍ 22.00 ♎

☊ 17.00

☾ 09.10

No Planting

X

Saturday 30
Before noon, sow wallflowers and Sweet Williams for next year and set out seedlings of other biennials.

♎

☾ 10.10

☾ ✶ ☉ 23.10

Sunday 31

♎

☾ 11.20

☾ ☌ ♄ 19.00

♈	♉	♊	♋	♌	♍
Aries	Taurus	Gemini	Cancer	Leo	Virgo
Fire	*Earth*	*Air*	*Water*	*Fire*	*Earth*

September 2014

Monday 1

♎ 07.00 ♏
◑
☾ 12.20

Change 07.00

Tuesday 2

Use the moonrise hour of 1 pm to take cuttings of cherry, laurel and privet, and prepare sites for new lawns.

♏
☾ 13.30

Wednesday 3

♏ 13.00 ♐
☾ 14.30
☾ △ ♀ 18.00

Change 13.00

Thursday 4

Pick early apples and pears while slightly under-ripe, and transplant or work on any fruit crops. Farmers, harvest the golden grain.

♐
☾ 15.20
☾ △ ☉ 18.40

Friday 5

♐ 15.00 ♑
☾ 16.10

Change 15.00

Saturday 6

A good day to prepare the soil. In the afternoon, sow winter radishes and harvest onions when the tops have died down.

♑
☾ 16.50

Sunday 7

♑ 15.00 ♒
☾ 17.20

Change 15.00

♎	♏	♐	♑	♒	♓
Libra	Scorpio	Sagittarius	Capricorn	Aquarius	Pisces
Air	*Water*	*Fire*	*Earth*	*Air*	*Water*

September 2014

Monday 8

Harvest now for ripe crops going straight to market. Perigee at Full Moon means a danger of flooding.

♒

℗ 04.00

☾ 17.50

PM only

Tuesday 9

At dusk, see the golden orb of the Harvest Moon. How large and low it appears amongst the autumn mists.

♒ 15.00 ♓

○ 02.00

☾ 18.20

Change 15.00

Wednesday 10

♓

☽ 08.00

Thursday 11

♓ 16.00 ♈

☊ 10.00

☽ 09.30

No Planting

Friday 12

♈

☽ 10.50

☽ △ ♀ 16.00

Saturday 13

An excellent day for fruit trees, with Sun–Moon trine, plus Moon–Saturn opposition.

♈ 20.00 ♉

☽ 12.00

☽ △ ⊙ 13.30

Sunday 14

Harvest Festival is celebrated this Sunday, with a harvest feast at the farmer's house. Make a corn dolly from the last sheaf of corn harvested.

♉

☽ 13.00

| ♄ Saturn | ⊙ Sun | ☍ Opposition | ✳ Sextile |
| ♀ Venus | ☌ Conjunction | □ Square | △ Trine |

September 2014

Monday 15

Lift and store potatoes, beets and carrots.

☿

☽ 14.00

Tuesday 16

Scatter wood ash on to rose beds and hoe it, preferably around 3 pm. Start planting bulbs today as well.

☿ 05.00 ♊

◑

☽ 14.50

Wednesday 17

Venus fades away as the Morning Star today.

♊

☽ 15.40

☽ ✳ ♀ 21.10

Thursday 18

♊ 16.00 ♋

☽ 16.10

☽ ✳ ☉ 18.40

Change 16.00

Friday 19

♋

☽ 16.50

Saturday 20

Sow parsley and chervil, and varieties of lettuce for overwintering under cloches.

♋

𝒜 14.00

☽ 17.10

Sunday 21

♋ 05.00 ♌

☽ 17.40

☽ ✳ ♄ 13.00

● New Moon   ◑ 1st quarter   ☾ Moonrise   ☊ North node   𝒜 Apogee

○ Full Moon   ◐ 3rd quarter   ☽ Moonset   ☋ South node   𝑃 Perigee

September 2014

Monday 22

Farmers: for best storage, harvest the ripe grain on the days coming up to this Harvest Moon.

♌

☽ 18.10

Tuesday 23

Honour the Autumn Equinox by telling the seasonal story of Demeter and Persephone.

♌ 17.00 ♍

☽ 18.20

☽ ✶ ♄ 07.40

Change 17.00

Wednesday 24

♍

● 06.00

☾ 06.00

PM only

Thursday 25

Jewish New Year.

♍

☋ 20.00

☾ 07.00

AM only

Friday 26

The Islamic month of *Zulhijah* begins.

♍ 04.00 ♎

☾ 08.10

Saturday 27

Use the moonrise hour to sow annuals in the greenhouse for a spring display.

♎

☾ 09.20

Sunday 28

♎ 13.00 ♏

☾ 10.20

☾ ✶ ♀ 20.30

Change 13.00

♈	♉	♊	♋	♌	♍
Aries	Taurus	Gemini	Cancer	Leo	Virgo
Fire	*Earth*	*Air*	*Water*	*Fire*	*Earth*

September 2014

Monday 29

Prune trees in the waning moon.

♏

☾ 11.20

☾ ⚹ ☉ 10.10

Tuesday 30

♏ 19.00 ♐

☾ 12.20

Change 19.00

Gardening Notes

♎
Libra
Air

♏
Scorpio
Water

♐
Sagittarius
Fire

♑
Capricorn
Earth

♒
Aquarius
Air

♓
Pisces
Water

October 2014

October Reminders

Wednesday 1 Pick late tomatoes or bring indoors to ripen if frost is forecast.	♐ ☾ 13.20	
Thursday 2	♐ 23.00 ♑ ☾ 14.10 ☾ ✶ ♄ 16.10	
Friday 3 A good day for preparing land and for digging compost into the soil.	♑ ☾ 14.50 ☾ △ ♀ 15.50	
Saturday 4	♑ ☾ 15.20	
Sunday 5	♑ 00.00 ♒ ☾ 15.50	

♄ Saturn	☉ Sun	☍ Opposition	✶ Sextile
♀ Venus	☌ Conjunction	☐ Square	△ Trine

October 2014

Monday 6

≈

℘ 10.00

☽ 16.20

No Planting

✗

Tuesday 7

Start planting winter lettuce around 4 pm, and force-grow rhubarb in a warm greenhouse.

≈ 01.00 ♓

☽ 16.50

Wednesday 8

This is the 'Hunter's Moon' and it's near perigee, so watch out for flooding. A total lunar eclipse is visible on the other side of the world.

♓

○ 11.00

☊ 18.00

☽ 17.20

No Planting

✗

Thursday 9

♓ 03.00 ♈

☽ 08.20

Friday 10

Continue to pick late tomatoes and let them ripen in trays. Work on any fruit trees, especially between 9–10 am.

♈

☽ 09.40

Saturday 11

♈ 06.00 ♉

☽ 10.50

Change 06.00

Sunday 12

♉

☽ 11.50

● New Moon	◐ 1st quarter	☽ Moonrise	☊ North node	⌐ Apogee
○ Full Moon	◑ 3rd quarter	☾ Moonset	☋ South node	℘ Perigee

October 2014

Monday 13

♉ 13.00 ♊

☽ 12.40

Change 13.00

Tuesday 14

♊

Prune rambling roses and plant out bulbs on rock gardens or between herbaceous plants this afternoon.

☽ 13.30

Wednesday 15

♊ 24.00 ♋

Work on roses and perennial flowers in the afternoon.

☽ 14.10

Thursday 16

♋

◑

The Sun meets the fixed star Spica today, associated with abundance, prosperity and good fortune.

☽ 14.50

Friday 17

♋

☽ 15.20

Saturday 18

♋ 12.00 ♌

𝒜 06.00

☽ 15.40

☽ ✶ ♀ 09.10

Change 12.00

Sunday 19

♌

☽ 16.10

☽ ✶ ☉ 13.10

♈	♉	♊	♋	♌	♍
Aries	Taurus	Gemini	Cancer	Leo	Virgo
Fire	Earth	Air	Water	Fire	Earth

October 2014

Monday 20
Continue to pick late tomatoes and let them ripen on trays.

♌

☽ 16.30

☽ ✳ ♄ 20.30

Tuesday 21
Dig up maincrop potatoes and lift and store beetroot.

♌ 00.00 ♍

☽ 16.50

Wednesday 22
At the dark of the Moon, pick crops to store over winter: potatoes, carrots and beetroot.

♍

☊ 24.00

☽ 17.20

AM only

Thursday 23
The Hindu festival of *Diwali* begins, on a partial lunar eclipse.

♍ 11.00 ♎

● 19.00

☾ 06.00

AM only

Friday 24
Prepare new rose-beds for planting, or plant lily of the valley.

♎

☾ 07.00

Saturday 25
It's the Islamic New Year, as the first month of *Muharram* begins.

♎ 19.00 ♏

☾ 08.10

☾ ☌ ♄ 16.10

Change 19.00

Sunday 26
British Summer Time ends.

♏

☾ 09.20

♎	♏	♐	♑	♒	♓
Libra	Scorpio	Sagittarius	Capricorn	Aquarius	Pisces
Air	*Water*	*Fire*	*Earth*	*Air*	*Water*

October 2014

Monday 27

Plant herbaceous perennials and deciduous trees, but avoid frosty conditions.

♏

☾ 10.20

Tuesday 28

♏ 00.00 ♐

☾ 11.20

☾ ✳ ☉ 19.10

Wednesday 29

Graft fruit trees and cut out fruited blackberry and loganberry canes.

♐

☾ 12.00

Thursday 30

♐ 04.00 ♑

☾ 12.50

Friday 31

Hallowe'en, traditionally a time of other-worldly interference in human affairs.

♑

◑

☾ 13.20

Gardening Notes

November 2014

November Reminders ─────────────

Saturday 1

♑ 07.00 ♒

☽ 14.00

Change 07.00

Sunday 2

♒

☽ 14.20

☽ △ ☉ 09.10   ☽ △ ♀ 13.00

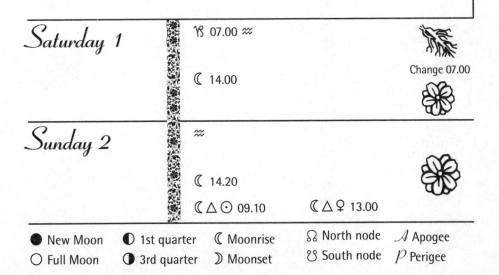

● New Moon	◑ 1st quarter	☾ Moonrise	☊ North node ⒜ Apogee
○ Full Moon	◐ 3rd quarter	☽ Moonset	☋ South node ⒫ Perigee

November 2014

Monday 3

≈ 10.00 ♓

♇ 00.00

☾ 14.50

PM only

Tuesday 4

Use the moonrise hour to lift chicory and asparagus.

♓

☾ 15.20

Wednesday 5

Bonfire night.

♓ 12.00 ♈

☊ 01.00

☾ 15.50

PM only

Thursday 6

♈

○ 22.00

☾ 16.20

Friday 7

The pagan quarter-day of Samhain, a gathering of the clans before winter.

♈ 16.00 ♉

☽ 07.20

Change 16.00

Saturday 8

♉

☽ 08.30

Sunday 9

♉ 22.00 ♊

☽ 09.30

♈	♉	♊	♋	♌	♍
Aries	Taurus	Gemini	Cancer	Leo	Virgo
Fire	*Earth*	*Air*	*Water*	*Fire*	*Earth*

November 2014

Monday 10

♊

☽ 10.20

Tuesday 11

♊

☽ 11.10

Wednesday 12

♊ 08.00 ♋

☽ 11.50

☽ △ ♀ 07.40

Change 08.00

Thursday 13

Clear fallen leaves and pile up for leaf mould.

♋

☽ 12.20

Friday 14

♋ 20.00 ♌

◑

☽ 12.40

Saturday 15

Sow broad beans if the soil is dry and over-winter under cloches.

♌

𝒜 02.00

☽ 13.10

Sunday 16

♌

☽ 13.30

♎	♏	♐	♑	♒	♓
Libra	Scorpio	Sagittarius	Capricorn	Aquarius	Pisces
Air	*Water*	*Fire*	*Earth*	*Air*	*Water*

November 2014

Monday 17

♌ 09.00 ♍

☽ 13.50

☽ ✶ ☉ 09.30

Change 09.00

Tuesday 18

♍

☽ 14.20

☉ ☌ ♄ 08.50

Wednesday 19

♍ 19.00 ♎

♌ 05.00

☽ 14.50

PM only

Thursday 20

Prick out any perennials you have raised in the greenhouse and sow winter bedding plants.

♎

☽ 15.10

Friday 21

♎

☽ 15.50

Saturday 22

Pick herbs to dry. Take cuttings of bay and rue and place in pots of sand. Re-pot mint in the greenhouse.

♎ 02.00 ♏

● 12.00

☾ 07.00

Sunday 23

Make a compost bin for the leaves you rake up in the garden. The Islamic month of *Safar* begins.

♏

☾ 08.10

| ♄ Saturn | ☉ Sun | ☌ Opposition | ✶ Sextile |
| ♀ Venus | ● Conjunction | □ Square | △ Trine |

November 2014

Monday 24

♏ 07.00 ♐

☾ 09.10

Change 07.00

Tuesday 25

Plant fruit trees and bushes, soak dry tree roots before planting, and prune fruit trees after planting. Stake trees.

♐

☾ 10.00

Wednesday 26

♐ 10.00 ♑

☾ 10.50

☾ ✶ ♄ 14.10

Change 10.00

Thursday 27

Trim the growth of globe artichokes and draw soil around the crowns. Turn over half-rotted compost and cover heavy land with rotted-down compost.

♑

℘ 22.00

☾ 11.30

☾ ✶ ♀ 18.40

AM only

Friday 28

Thanksgiving (USA).

♑ 13.00 ♒

☾ 12.00

Change 13.00

Saturday 29

Prick out any perennials you have raised in the greenhouse and sow winter bedding plants.

♒

◑

☾ 12.30

Sunday 30

St Andrew's Day.
First Sunday in Advent.

♒ 16.00 ♓

☾ 13.00

Change 16.00

● New Moon	◑ 1st quarter	☾ Moonrise	☊ North node	𝒜 Apogee
○ Full Moon	◐ 3rd quarter	☽ Moonset	☋ South node	℘ Perigee

December 2014

Monday 1
♓

☽ 13.20
☽ △ ☉ 17.30

Tuesday 2
♓ 20.00 ♈
☊ 06.00

☽ 13.50
☽ △ ♀ 11.00

PM only

Wednesday 3
♈

☽ 14.20

Thursday 4
Venus appears as the Evening Star.
♈

☽ 15.00

Friday 5
Check over any stored corns or tubers for signs of mould.
♈ 01.00 ♉

☽ 15.40

Saturday 6
St Michael's Day falls on Full Moon. See how high this rises into the night sky.
♉

○ 12.00
☽ 16.20

Sunday 7
♉ 07.00 ♊

☽ 08.10
☽ ☌ ♀ 09.50

Change 07.00

♈	♉	♊	♋	♌	♍
Aries	Taurus	Gemini	Cancer	Leo	Virgo
Fire	*Earth*	*Air*	*Water*	*Fire*	*Earth*

December 2014

Monday 8
Pot on autumn-sown sweet peas.

♊

☽ 09.00

Tuesday 9

♊ 17.00 ♋

☽ 09.40

Change 17.00

Wednesday 10
Plant new hedges, shrubs and trees.

♋

☽ 10.20

Thursday 11

♋

☽ 10.50

☽ △ ☉ 18.10

Friday 12

♋ 04.00 ♌

𝒜 22.00

☽ 11.10

Saturday 13
Sow carrots in frames.

♌

☽ 11.40

Sunday 14
Geminid meteor shower.

♌ 17.00 ♍

◑

☽ 12.00

Change 17.00

♎	♏	♐	♑	♒	♓
Libra	Scorpio	Sagittarius	Capricorn	Aquarius	Pisces
Air	*Water*	*Fire*	*Earth*	*Air*	*Water*

December 2014

Monday 15
Dispose of soft vegetable waste by digging it into trenches.

♍

☽ 12.20

Tuesday 16
♍

♌ 11.00

☽ 12.50

No Planting

✗

Wednesday 17
♍ 04.00 ♎

☽ 13.10

☽ ✶ ☉ 05.40

Thursday 18
A fine Flower day. Sow in the greenhouse around noon. Prune back established rose-beds. Plant shrubs if weather permits.

♎

☽ 13.40

☽ ✶ ♀ 09.00

Friday 19
♎ 12.00 ♏

☽ 14.20

Change 12.00

Saturday 20
Trim back lawn-edges to make the garden tidy.

♏

☽ 15.00

Sunday 21
Winter Solstice – the longest night. The Sun crosses over the Galactic Equator.

♏ 16.00 ♐

☽ 15.50

Change 16.00

♄ Saturn   ☉ Sun   ☍ Opposition   ✶ Sextile

♀ Venus   ☌ Conjunction   ☐ Square   △ Trine

December 2014

Monday 22

Sow melons for an early crop, and early peas and dwarf beans for cropping under glass.

♐

● 01.00

☾ 07.50

Tuesday 23

♐ 18.00 ♑

☾ 08.40

Change 18.00

Wednesday 24

♑

P 16.00

☾ 09.30

No Planting

✗

Thursday 25

Christmas Day.

♑ 19.00 ♒

☾ 10.00

Change 19.00

Friday 26

A harmonious Sun–Sextile Moon chimes for Boxing Day.

♒

☾ 10.30

☾ ✶ ☉ 11.50

Saturday 27

A good Flower day with the Moon–Venus aspect, tend to indoor flowers.

♒ 21.00 ♓

☾ 11.00

☾ ✶ ♀ 15.40

Sunday 28

♓

☾ 11.30

● New Moon	◑ 1st quarter	☾ Moonrise	☊ North node	A Apogee
○ Full Moon	◐ 3rd quarter	☽ Moonset	☋ South node	P Perigee

December 2014

Monday 29

♓

☽ (half moon)   ☊ 09.00

☾ 12.00

No Planting

✗

Tuesday 30

♓ 01.00 ♈

☾ 12.30

Wednesday 31
New Year's Eve.

♈

☾ 13.00

Gardening Notes —————————————————

♈	♉	♊	♋	♌	♍
Aries	Taurus	Gemini	Cancer	Leo	Virgo
Fire	*Earth*	*Air*	*Water*	*Fire*	*Earth*

The Seasons of 2014

Young Spring was there, his head encircled with a flowery garland, and Summer, lightly clad, crowned with a wreath of corn ears; Autumn too, stained purple with treading out the vintage, and icy Winter, with white and shaggy locks.

Ovid

Imbolc, or winter's end, when the first glimpse of spring appears, has the Christian name of Candlemas, and falls on 3 February. The fertility-festival of Beltane at the beginning of May heralds the change from spring to summer, and then Lammas in August signifies the end of summer and the start of autumn. Autumn ends at Samhain (pronounced 'sawain'). Some say that the nearest New Moons to Imbolc and Samhain and nearest Full Moons for Beltane and Lammas, were used for festival and ceremony. A revived interest in these old 'fire-festivals' now brings us into closer contact with the natural passage of the year.

These quarter-days arrive when the Sun reaches 15° of the fixed signs, for instance 15° Scorpio for Imbolc, so they are midway between solstice and equinox – don't let your friends tell you they happen on the first day of the month! That loses their cosmic meaning, and these festivals existed long before the solar months. Tuning into the eightfold structure of the solar year, we honour Beltane on 5 May and Lammas on 7 August.

At Beltane, the traditional time when livestock were put out to pasture, one should be up to greet the dawn, after an all-night party if you like. The word 'Lammas' alludes to the loaf made from the new wheat. It's a holiday summer's-end festival at the start of the harvest. Our modern equivalent of Samhain, the start of the Celtic New Year, is Hallowe'en. As Nature dies, it brings an other-worldly flavour as a time of supernatural interference in human affairs: ghosts, ghouls and divination, 'mischief night', a time for the clans to meet. The solstices and equinoxes are here given to the hour. This calendar isn't interested in dates that are fixed by the calendar months: those defined by the Sun and Moon are more fun.

The year begins with Venus rising in the East as the Morning Star, which was called, Lucifer. In old English this was called Éarendel, and Tolkein in his ring mythology had more or less the same name: 'Hail Eärendil, bearer of light before the Sun and Moon'. The Morning-star announces the arrival of the Sun, is the harbinger of the day to come and stands at the breaking of dawn as the last star to disappear into the glory of the Sun. Try to spot Venus appearing before the Sun in the early morning around 16 January, then watch as it grows most brilliant in early February, then rising highest in the sky mid-March. Later in the year it will fade away into the rising Sun in mid-September – it is supposed to stay visible in the sky for 263 days altogether, which is the duration of human gestation; then it will re-appear as the Evening Star above the sunset on 4 December.

Sacred Moons of 2014

Here are the sacred Moons that are celebrated around the world in 2014, the Full Moons of Easter and Wesak (Buddhist) plus other New Moon festivals.

Chinese New Year	31 January, Year of Horse	New Moon on 30 January
Mardi Gras	4 March	New Moon on 1 March
Hindu New Year	31 March	New Moon on 30 March
Easter Sunday	20 April	Full Moon on 15 April
Buddhist Wesak	14 May	Full Moon on 14 May
Start of Ramadan	28 June	New Moon on 27 June
Jewish New Year	25 September	New Moon on 24 September
Hindu Diwali	23 October	New Moon on 23 October
Muslim New Year	25 October	New Moon on 23 October

This year the Chinese New Year is near to the pagan quarter-day of Imbolc on 3 February, as it should be. Imbolc is between the winter solstice and the spring equinox. Surely this is the best time to start the New Year, on the New Moon nearest to this quarter-day, where Imbolc signifies the first promise of spring? In contrast, Mardi Gras chimes rather late on 4 March.

Schoolchildren today learn to celebrate and respect the festivals of all the major faiths, as well as events in diverse cultures. In turn, it makes sense to also honour the *sacred Moons* on which these ceremonies are based. These are either Full or New, sometimes a day or two after New Moon, when the first thin crescent is glimpsed at dawn or dusk. The calendars of the great religions were founded on the lunar cycle, and lunar-based sacred calendars still have the force of living custom among peoples of the world. Sensibly, a new year begins on a New Moon – the proper time for new beginnings. Our table gives the dates for five world religions – Islam, Judaism, Christianity, Buddhism and Hinduism – plus the Chinese State calendar and Mardi Gras (Fat Tuesday), the time of wild celebration in Brazil before the beginning of Lent. The honouring of these sacred Moons of different cultures can be a socially cohesive force in the modern world.

Our calendar months were originally lunar, and still are in the Jewish and Muslim calendars. To keep in step with the solar year, a 13th month is added every third year. Muslims don't do this, so their year has only 12 lunar months, and moves round by 11 days every year, moving slowly backwards against the solar year. The two calendars come together every 33 years. *Ramadan*, the ninth month in the Muslim year, is in June, following the New Moon on 27 June. Muslims experience the start of the month, beginning one or two days after the calendrical

New Moons: they see the thin crescent of the New Moon in the evening sky when their month begins. Thus their New Year stars on 25 October in 2014, after the New Moon two days previously.

The *Eid al-Fitr* festival for the end of *Ramadan* probably falls on 28 July, starting the evening before – it can vary with location depending upon when the Moon is seen. Old wrongs are forgiven and money is given to the poor, with Muslims getting up early to pray and wearing fine clothes.

The sensible Chinese start their new year around early February, reflecting the fact that life begins in darkness, as a seed germinates in the dark womb of the Earth. The 'dark' time of the month when no Moon is visible, in the dark and cold time of the year (January/ February), is an appropriate time for this important celebration of *beginning*. 2014 is the Year of the Horse in the circle of twelve years. That's the Chinese version of the Jupiter cycle, as it spends a year in front of each of the twelve zodiac constellations. On New Year's Day, the Chinese clear out clutter, pay off debts and, with the aid of a dragon, chase away the winter blues.

Christianity has rather suppressed the lunar calendar, except for Easter, where Easter Sunday is that following the first Full Moon after the spring equinox. One celebrates the burgeoning forces of spring and renewal on Easter Sunday. Lent begins (following Shrove Tuesday) six weeks before Easter Sunday, 5 March 2014. This is the only way in which Christendom follows the rhythm of the lunar months.

Buddhism didn't conquer nations, so it does not impose a single New Year's Day. The day Buddhists celebrate it varies in different Buddhist states. There is, however, a major Full Moon festival for Buddha's birthday, called *Wesak*, which falls on 14 May 2014, two lunar months after the Easter Full Moon. Jewish New Year begins on the New Moon before the autumn equinox, on 25 September.

Diwali, the Indian 'Festival of Lights', falls a couple of months later and this year this falls on 23 October. Although it falls late in the year, *Diwali* may have originated as a harvest festival, signifying the last harvest of the year before winter. It's a five-day Indian New Moon festival and this is the middle day – wish your family and friends *Shubh Diwali!* and light candles. This festival thanks the deity of wealth and abundance, the Hindu Goddess Lakshmi. It falls on the New Moon nearest to the quarter-day we call Samhain.

In times gone by, sages wisely fixed these festival-dates on New Moons, anchored to the quarter-days. Through these sacred events one can experience the concept of the New Moon as a beginning. In ancient Greece the wedding-month of *Gamelia*, January/February, pertained especially to the New Moon of that month. 'Monogamy' derives from this old word. Thus marriages were made in the dark time of the year and of the month. Things start to grow in the darkness, like a seed sprouting under the soil. In today's electric-light society one is hardly able to sense the significance of this time of the month when the Moon cannot be seen by day or night. Mental health, balance in life and happiness are all assisted by living more in tune with the lunar month.

Further Reading

Barger, Adèle, *Gardening Success with Lunar Aspects*, American Federation of Astrologers, 1977.

Biodynamics: *New Directions for Farming and Gardening in New Zealand*, Random Century, N.Z., 1989.

Burns, J.T., *Cosmic Influences on Humans, Animals and Plants, An Annotated Bibliography*, Magill (US), 1997.

Culpeper, N., *Culpeper's Complete Herbal*, Foulsham, London.

Dariotus Redivivus, or a brief introduction to the judgement of the stars, 1653 (agricultural section by Nathaniel Spark).

Domin, A., Ed., *Organic Wholefoods, Naturally Delicious Cuisine*, Konemann, 1997.

Elliott, Jean, *Plants and Planets, Astrological Gardening*, self-published, 1996.

Estienne, C. & Liebault, J., *La Maison Rustique*, trans. Surfleet, 1616.

Gauquelin, Michel, *The Cosmic Clocks*, Pan Books, 1969.

Hill, T., *The Gardener's Labyrinth*, 1577, OUP, 1987.

Joly, N., *Le Vin du Ciel à la Terre*, Paris, 1997.

Kolisko, L., *Agriculture of Tomorrow*, Kolisko Archive Publications, Bournemouth, 1939, 1982.

Kollerstrom, N. & Power, C., 'The influence of the lunar cycle on fertility on two thoroughbred studfarms', *Equine Fertility Journal*, 2000, 32, 75–77.

Kollerstrom, N. & Staudenmaier, G., 'Evidence for Lunar-Sidereal Rhythms in Crop Yield: A Review', *Biological Agriculture and Horticulture 2001*, 19, 247–259.

Lieber, A. L., *The Lunar Effect*, Corgi, 1979.

Playfair, G. & Hill, S., *The Cycles of Heaven*, Pan Books, 1979.

Pliny, *History of Nature*, Vol. 18, Section 75 (Loeb Classics, 1961).

Podolinsky, A., *Bio-Dynamic Agriculture Introductory Lectures*, Vol.1, Australia, 1990.

Powell, R. & Treadgold, P., *The Sidereal Zodiac*, Anthroposophical Publications, US, 1979.

Sattler, F. & Wistinghausen, E., *Bio-Dynamic Farming Practice*, CUP, 1989.

Shaw, Beth, 'Landmarks of the year', *Astrological Journal*, April 1997, 26–35. (Invaluable advice on seasons and festivals.)

Taylor, Peter, Chill, A Reassessment of Global Warming Theory, Clairview Books, 2009.

Temple, J., *Gardening Without Chemicals*, 1986.

Thun, M., *Gardening for Life*, Hawthorne Press, 2000.

Thun, M., *Results from the Biodynamic Sowing and Planting Calendar*, Floris Books, 2003.

Thun, M. and M., *When Wine Tastes Best*, Floris Books, 2009.

$\mathcal{I}ndex$